Your Towns and Cities in t

Winchester
in the Great War

Your Towns and Cities in the Great War

Winchester
in the Great War

John J Eddleston

Pen & Sword
MILITARY

First published in Great Britain in 2016 by
PEN & SWORD MILITARY
an imprint of
Pen and Sword Books Ltd
47 Church Street
Barnsley
South Yorkshire S70 2AS

ISBN 978 1 78346 329 9

A CIP record for this book is available from the British Library

Printed and bound in England
by CPI Group (UK) Ltd, Croydon, CR0 4YY

Typeset in Times New Roman by Chic Graphics

Pen & Sword Books Ltd incorporates the imprints of
Pen & Sword Archaeology, Atlas, Aviation, Battleground, Discovery,
Family History, History, Maritime, Military, Naval, Politics,
Railways, Select, Social History, Transport, True Crime, Claymore
Press, Frontline Books, Leo Cooper, Praetorian Press, Remember
When, Seaforth Publishing and Wharncliffe.

For a complete list of Pen and Sword titles please contact
Pen and Sword Books Limited
47 Church Street, Barnsley, South Yorkshire, S70 2AS, England
E-mail: enquiries@pen-and-sword.co.uk
Website: www.pen-and-sword.co.uk

Contents

Introduction

The city of Winchester is an ancient city. There is evidence of settlement in the area in prehistoric times but it increased in importance at the time of the Roman conquest when it became the capital city of the local tribe, the Belgae and as such was named Venta Belgarum.

A link with these early times was discovered in 2000 when a hoard of Iron Age jewellery was found buried in a field close to the city. The find was declared treasure trove and valued at £350,000, the highest reward up to that time under the Treasure Act of 1966.

Like many other cities and towns, Winchester began to decline after the departure of the Romans but when England was divided into various Anglo-Saxon kingdoms, Winchester became the capital of Wessex towards the end of the seventh century.

In the ninth century, Winchester's bishop was one Swithun who died in the early 860s. Swithun was buried somewhere outside his church, at his own request, supposedly so his body would be subject to the feet of passers-by and the raindrops falling from the heavens. In 971 his body was moved inside the church and, coincidentally, it rained heavily on that day, a sign that the venerable man was displeased with the move and the legend grew that if it rained on his feast day, 15 July, it would continue to do so for the next forty days.

Once the kingdom of Wessex had unified the other kingdoms such as East Anglia and Mercia into what we now know as England, Winchester became a capital of England, which it remained until after the Norman Conquest in 1066.

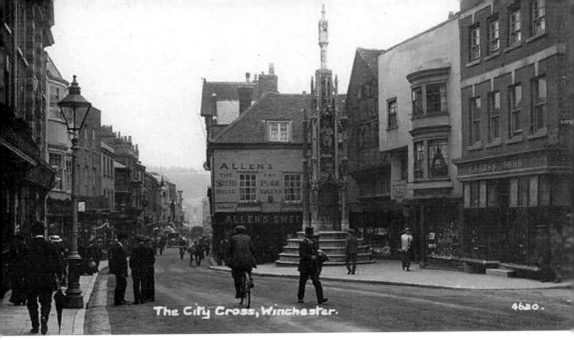

A view of the City Cross towards the end of the war.

In 1141 a terrible fire destroyed a great part of the city and led to its steady decline. However, the fourteenth-century Bishop of Winchester, William of Wykeham, greatly helped the city's restoration and founded the famous college.

The famous Pilgrim's Way, to Canterbury began at Winchester and not in London as many might think. The City Cross has stood in the High Street for over six hundred years. It was purchased by one Thomas Dummer in 1770, who intended to dismantle it and have it re-erected at his country home. A local riot prevented the move and the cross remained where it was.

A number of famous people are buried in the Cathedral including some Anglo-Saxon kings, such as Egbert, along with later rulers, such as King Canute and the second Norman king, William II. Jane Austen, the author, is also buried there.

Many famous people have been born in Winchester, including Arthur, Prince of Wales who was King VII's eldest son. He died before his father so never became king but his wife, Catherine of Aragon, then married Arthur's brother, who became King Henry VIII. Another king, Henry III, was born at Winchester in 1207. Two years later, in 1209, Richard, Earl of Cornwall, the younger brother of the future Henry III and who was elected King of the Romans in 1257, was also born in Winchester.

The city is an ancient settlement with many royal connections and a historic significance in social, economic and political events. Although far from being the centre of political life in 1914, nor one noted for massive heavy industrial output, it still played a not insignificant part in Britain's war effort. Over the years Winchester has become an important military centre and this aspect comes to the fore in the war years.

CHAPTER 1

The Lull Before the Storm

1914 opened in Winchester as any other year. The weather was unduly cold and a good deal of snow fell in the area but, for the most part, life went on as it always had before.

Politics and education were in the news in January. On the 14th of that month the headmaster of Winchester School, Mr MJ Rendall, acted as the first speaker in a group of educationalists who made representations to the Prime Minister. In fact, Mr Asquith was in France when the deputation arrived in London, so the group had to make do with Mr JA Pease. Their concern was that any further grants of public money earmarked in the forthcoming Education Bill, should be spent to improve staffing in schools and to increase the basic stipend of teachers. Mr Pease said that he would pass the concerns on to Mr Asquith when he returned to London.

Five days after this, on 19 January, another educational establishment was in the news, but for very different reasons. A burglary took place at Winton House, a school for boys on the outskirts of Winchester. The intruder left behind a loaded revolver, a pair of galoshes and a pair of gloves but had taken a banjo case into which he had crammed a number of silver items including several cream jugs, a Dutch model of a ship, an ornament of a milkmaid with two buckets, a pepper mill shaped like a milk churn, a Queen Anne mustard pot, two large cups and a number of cigarette cases. The only other clues the police had was that a man carrying a banjo case was seen heading towards Winchester railway station and inquiries showed that he had then purchased a single ticket to Waterloo. The investigation then moved to London where, on 23 January, officers found that the items had been sold to a jeweller, but the man had given a false name and address and the trail soon ran cold.

The month of February seemed to be one for the law courts. On the 10th of the month Mister Justice Ridley, sitting at the Winchester Assizes, sentenced William Joshua Woollacott to three years' imprisonment. Woollacott was a railway carriage examiner at Bournemouth and was found guilty of stealing luggage from passengers. Though he pleaded guilty to four specimen charges, it was believed that he had committed many more offences over a number of years.

The following day a more complex case opened at the same court. Three members of the same family, Florence Louise Way and her parents, Bertie and Elizabeth, were charged with obtaining £800 by false pretences from Annie Maria Wheeler and her husband William. The story was a most curious one, which the press dubbed the 'Musical Millions' case.

Florence, it seems, was a musical student and had told Annie Wheeler that some of her compositions had been accepted by a major American syndicate. They were going to publish her music and the payment for the work would amount to around a million pounds. There was, however, a minor problem, in that she had to pay for various licences and contracts. Florence told this story to Annie and William Wheeler who then advanced her various small sums of money until the total amounted to some £800.

The story only came to light when William Wheeler, having given out so much money, found himself unable to pay his bills and had to file for bankruptcy. Florence Way's story was checked by the authorities and shown to be a pack of lies. She was arrested and later her parents were also taken into custody, the police believing that they had benefitted from the fraud and so were also guilty.

When the trial opened, Florence pleaded guilty to thirty-three counts of obtaining money by false pretences; but both Bertie and Elizabeth pleaded not guilty. The case continued until 19 February when Bertie was acquitted by the jury. Elizabeth, though, was found to be guilty as charged. Florence was sentenced to eighteen months in prison and Elizabeth received twelve months but, because she had pleaded not guilty, her sentence was one of a year with hard labour.

There was also a local tragedy in February. John Thomas Philip Drew once served as the Superintendent of the Prudential Society at Winchester but had, some months previously, been sent to Moseley, in Birmingham, to serve in a similar position. Drew was not happy in his new post and so, on 19 February, returned to Winchester, where he lay down on the railway line. His decapitated body was found by a platelayer on his way to work.

Military news hit the headlines in March. On the 2nd of the month figures were released by the British Army detailing the number of men who had joined up for the year ending 30 September 1913. The figures were very disappointing, showing that only 28,691 men had joined, a fall of 2,225 on the previous year. Almost every region had seen a fall but a few had seen a slight rise. The greatest rise of all was in the 37th District, which was Winchester, where 1,030 men had joined.

An interesting snippet later in the month referred back to the news of a century before, which reported that at the Winchester Assizes death sentences had been passed on one man for forgery, three foreigners for murder, one man for sheep stealing and one man for burglary. Only three of those men were later hanged. On 26 March 1814, Henry Worthington was hanged for forgery, Thomas Brown for burglary and Thomas Steel for sheep theft.

An amusing anecdote concerning the Bishop of Winchester appeared in the newspapers in April. The Bishop was riding his horse along a country lane when a small boy threw a stone at him. The Bishop reprimanded him, saying that God was a witness to all that he did. The boy asked if the Lord could see what he did in his grandmother's back kitchen. When the Bishop replied that He could, the boy grinned and said that this would be a good trick as his grandmother did not have a back kitchen.

The army was back in the news this month and not for a good reason. An officer, Captain Hugo Watson, who was stationed at Winchester, was fined £1 and bound over for six months for assaulting a corn merchant, Charles Adams, by punching him in the right eye. Captain Watson claimed that Mr Adams had insulted his wife but the bench ruled that this was no excuse for violence.

On 1 May, a terrible fire took place at a stables in Martyr Worthy, near Winchester. The stables were constructed from old railway sleepers and so burned furiously. Five thoroughbred yearling racing colts, belonging to Donald Nicoll, were roasted to death and only one horse, a stud stallion named Little Flutter, was saved. The financial loss was estimated at £5,000.

On 8 May, details of the forthcoming town crier competition were announced. The contest would be held at Marlborough, where Mr WB Angliss of that town would defend his title. The Winchester representative would be Mr W Hall.

Towards the end of the month, on 29 May, a large hoard of silver coins was discovered in the garden of Manor Farm, Itchen Abbas, near Winchester. There were a total of 234 coins, mainly half-crowns, shillings and sixpences, from the reigns of Elizabeth, James I and Charles I and it was believed that they had probably been hidden at some time during the Civil War. The coins were seized by the county police, pending a decision by the Coroner as to whether the items were treasure trove.

June was a month of bright sunshine and hot weather. On 3 June, the Coroner ruled on the Itchen Abbas hoard, stating that it was a matter to be sorted out between the owner of Manor Farm and the Treasury.

On the 13th of the month, Sir Herbert Maxwell unveiled a memorial window to Izaak Walton in Winchester cathedral. It was estimated that the cost of the window was close to £400.

There was further legal news in the month of June. One announcement was that Thomas Lynch had been released from Parkhurst prison on the Isle of Wight. Lynch, an elderly blind man, who had lived at the Winchester workhouse, was found guilty of the murder of a fellow inmate in 1906. Condemned to death, the sentence had later been commuted to one of life imprisonment.

Not so fortunate was another man sentenced to death, Walter James White. Walter had been very much in love with Frances Priscilla Hunter, who worked as a waitress at the Goddard Arms Hotel in Swindon. Marriage had been discussed and it was a proud and happy Walter who went to meet Frances's brother, who lived near Glamorgan.

That meeting went well but was marred by the fact that the landlady, Mrs Blewitt, flatly refused to let Frances into her house. Instead she took Walter to one side and said she would write to him later and explain the matter. Eventually, she told Walter that some time before Frances had lived with another man, as his wife, without actually being married to him.

Walter was of the old-fashioned school and wanted his wife to be a virgin when he married. This news devastated him, especially since Frances had not mentioned it to him herself. He brooded on the matter for some days before deciding that he wished to kill Frances and then himself.

On Wednesday, 29 April, Walter went to the Goddard Arms and

The Goddard Arms, where the murder of Frances Hunter took place.

asked Frances to step out into the yard with him. A few minutes later the manager of the hotel heard three shots. Rushing out to investigate, he found Frances lying dead in the coal house and Walter standing over her. Walter had not tried to kill himself and calmly waited for the police to arrive and take him into custody. Walter James White faced his trial at Winchester on 28 May and was duly found guilty of murder. Sentenced to death, he paid the ultimate price for his crime when he was hanged at Winchester prison on Tuesday, 16 June. It was already the fifth execution at the prison in the twentieth century.

Eight days after Walter White was hanged, on 28 June, initial reports of a shooting in Sarajevo reached the newspapers in Britain. The storm was about to erupt.

CHAPTER 2

The Road to War

Whilst it is true that the final catalyst to the Great War was the assassination of the heir to the Austro-Hungarian throne, Archduke Franz Ferdinand, on 28 June 1914, in Sarajevo by Gavrilo Princip, the real roots of the conflict lay in past events.

Before 1870, Germany did not exist as a state. Germany was a geographical term consisting of a number of small, medium and large states, the chief of which was Prussia. In 1866, a war between Prussia and Austria-Hungary resulted in a Prussian victory and increased dominance of Prussia. This was followed a few years later, in 1870, by the Franco-Prussian war, in which France was humiliated, losing the territories of Alsace and Lorraine. It also resulted in the unification of the various states into the Empire of Germany on 18 January 1871. The King of Prussia, Wilhelm I, became Emperor, or Kaiser, of the new Germany.

There had been a number of great powers within Europe. Britain was undoubtedly the strongest but there was also France, Russia, Austria-Hungary and the Ottoman Empire. The formation of a new great power, Germany, led to disquiet amongst some of these other powers, who sought to protect themselves by a system of alliances.

In 1879, Germany and Austria-Hungary agreed that they would support each other if either of them were attacked; in 1882 they were joined by the recently reunited Italy. This left the French feeling vulnerable. In 1882 she signed a formal military alliance with a most unlikely nation – Republican France allied herself with autocratic, Tsarist Russia. In 1904, the *Entente Cordiale* was signed between Britain and France. This was not one document but a series of agreements covering a range of issues that had or were causing tensions between the two nations. However, neither side made any formal military agreement, although there was a commitment to greater military cooperation. Britain resolved several problem areas with the Russians shortly afterwards; in 1907 it became a Triple Entente, which seemed to be facing against the Triple Alliance of the Central Powers.

For various reasons, the Balkans had become an area of considerable instability, especially in the last decade or so.

For some time, Russia had seen herself as the protector of the Slavic peoples and the interests of Russia (historic protector of the Slavs) and the Austria-Hungarians (protector of her Empire) clashed.

The visit of the Archduke Franz Ferdinand and his wife, Sophie, to Sarajevo on 28 June 1914, in part, to view military manoeuvres, was seen as an opportunity by Slav pro-nationalists, in particular by what may be called a terrorist group, the Black Hand, to strike a telling blow for the cause. The group was based in Serbia, the largest power amongst the relatively new Balkan States, eager to use its capabilities to enlarge its boundaries. Already in the twentieth century the Balkans had seen the cause of several major European crisis – always with Serbia as a major participant – and which has involved all the European powers. The Black Hand felt that the murder of Franz Ferdinand would provoke Austria-Hungary into drastic action and Russia, as protector of the Slavs, would be drawn into any resultant war. This seemed to be the quickest route to the establishments of a great Slav nation.

Six members of the Black Hand formed a group intent on killing Franz Ferdinand. As his car drove through the streets of the city a bomb was thrown but bounced off the car and injured a number of spectators. The Archduke was furious at the attempt on his life and insisted on visiting the injured in hospital. After the visit he climbed

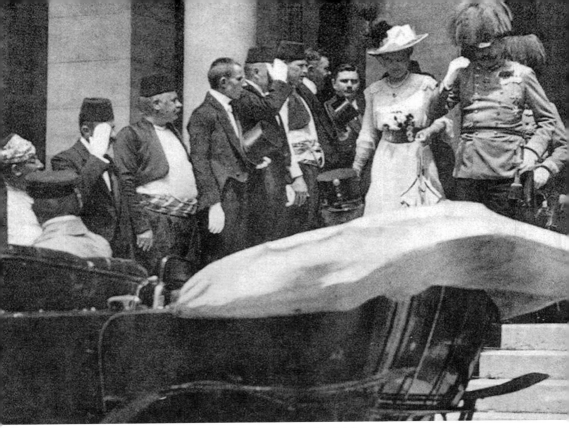

The Archduke and his wife in Sarajevo on the fateful day.

back into his car with the intention of continuing his official visit but the driver took a wrong turn. He reversed the car, which stalled. It was at that point that another of the assassins, Gavrilo Princip, stepped forward.

Two shots were fired from a distance of about five feet. One bullet struck Franz Ferdinand in the jugular vein and the second struck his wife, Sophie, in the abdomen. Both victims died that same day. The countdown to a major European war had started. One week after the assassination, on 5 July, the Austrian Emperor, Franz Joseph, wrote to the Kaiser, Wilhelm II, reminding him of the agreement between the two countries signed in 1879 and asking him to confirm that he would support Austria-Hungary in any intervention in Serbia. The Kaiser quickly agreed that Germany would offer whatever support was needed.

Archduke Franz Ferdinand's car on the Appel Quay, less than a minute from where the shooting took place.

The pistol used by Princip, the weapon that started the First World War.

Gavrilo Princip, the man who assassinated the Archduke and his wife.

The arrest of the assassin after the shooting.

Two weeks after this, on 23 July, Austria delivered an ultimatum to Serbia, one that would be almost impossible for Serbia to agree to. Five days later, on 28 July, Austria declared war on Serbia and the same day began to bombard Belgrade. This in turn brought Russia into the conflict. The Austrian ambassador was summoned and told that if its troops did not withdraw from Serbia, Russia would declare war.

Austria did not withdraw and the Russians started to mobilise their army. At the same time Russia called

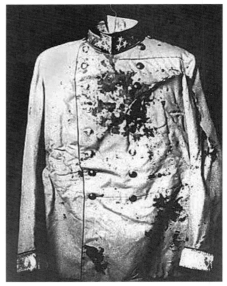

The tunic worn by Archduke Ferdinand when he was shot. Note the heavy bloodstaining.

DRASTIC GERMAN ULTIMATUM.

12 HOURS' TIME LIMIT TO RUSSIA.

A NOTE PRESENTED TO FRANCE.

INTERNATIONAL COMMUNICATIONS RESTRICTED.

THE KAISER SAYS GERMANY IS FORCED!

Speech ₋y the Kaiser : '' The Sword is Being Forced
Into Our Hands.''

The banner headlines in the newspapers before the war broke out.

upon France, reminded her of their agreement under the 1882 treaty, and asked her to join them in a war against Austria-Hungary.

Now it was Germany's turn to intervene. On 31 July, she demanded that Russia must stop her mobilisation or a state of war would exist between them. When Russia did not comply Germany declared war on her on 1 August.

Whilst all this was going on and the people of Winchester read each day that war seemed to be growing ever closer, life and death continued. On 6 July, an inquest opened on Rear Admiral Percy Ashe, who died from injuries sustained in a motorcycle accident on Saturday, 4 July. In fact, Admiral Ashe was involved in two accidents. He was riding his cycle from Winchester to Camberley when he suddenly swerved, ran up a dirt bank and overturned in a ditch. People came to his aid but the Rear Admiral said that he was unhurt and wished to continue his journey. He had only gone a few miles more when he approached a car driven by Mr H Baldwin. Suddenly, the motorcycle swerved and struck Mr Baldwin's vehicle in the side, killing Ashe immediately. Stating that he may have been affected by the first incident when he swerved into a ditch, the Coroner arrived at a verdict of accidental death.

Just over a week later, on 14 July, the Court of Appeal quashed the conviction of Richard Sagar, who had been sentenced to twelve months hard labour at the recent Winchester Assizes on a charge of false pretences. It appeared that the trial judge, Mister Justice Ridley, had refused to allow certain documents to be admitted into evidence and these had been essential for the defence.

As July ended many of the citizens of Winchester must have been concerned about the possibility of Britain becoming involved in a European conflagration; but there were positive signs. When the Cabinet debated the possibility of war, no fewer than five ministers had said that they would resign immediately if war came. It was true that we were partners in the Triple Entente but the entire affair was a dispute in the Balkans and had little or nothing to do with Britain. Peace could still be won.

In Germany, the authorities knew that now that they had declared war on Russia, it was almost certain that hostilities with France would follow. Such a war had been considered likely ever since the Franco-Prussian war and plans had been drawn up, accordingly. Rather than face the direct might of the French army, the Germans had created what has become known as the Schlieffen Plan, which involved attacking France through Belgium and Holland. It was believed that this would lead to a French defeat within six weeks. There was, however, a problem. In 1839 the Treaty of London, signed by Britain, Prussia and other countries, guaranteed the new state of Belgium's neutrality. It was for Germany to decide whether they could gamble on Britain not holding to that treaty.

In the event, on 3 August 1914, Germany declared war on France and that same day invaded Belgium to put the Schlieffen Plan into operation. Immediately Britain demanded that Germany withdraw her troops from Belgium and gave her until midnight on 4 August to comply. Germany stated that she would not accept the ultimatum; telegrams were sent out to the British Grand Fleet stating that it was to consider German shipping as hostile. Britain was now at war with Germany.

CHAPTER 3

5 August to the End of 1914

From the moment hostilities broke out, Winchester became a pivotal part of Britain's war effort. The nearest port was Southampton, designated Port Number One, from which most of the men and equipment would depart for France. Winchester was to form a major area for troop encampments before units were sent to Southampton for embarkation.

One of the very first casualties of the war was a namesake of the city. The SS *City of Winchester*, a merchant vessel, was captured by the German cruiser *Konigsberg* 280 miles from Aden, on its return home from India, and sunk on 6 August, just two days after war had been declared.

The next day, 7 August, a small part of the British Expeditionary Force arrived in France. The day after that, 8 August, fifty German prisoners were received at Winchester jail. They had been on a liner, which was berthed at Southampton when hostilities broke out; four of the prisoners were women.

TO DRESS EXTRAVAGANTLY IN WAR TIME IS WORSE THAN BAD FORM IT IS UNPATRIOTIC

One of the posters used during the war to encourage people to 'do their bit' in whatever way they could.

High Street, Winchester at about the time of the Great War.

The gate in Winchester in the early part of the twentieth century.

On 12 August, a further escalation came when Britain, as expected, declared war on Austria-Hungary. At about the same time the newspapers in Winchester announced that the Prince of Wales' National Relief Fund now stood at £1,315,000 and the Bishop of Winchester announced that he had offered his Episcopal residence, Farnham Castle, to the War Office for use as a hospital.

The first major British battle of the war opened on 23 August at Mons and this was followed three days later by the Battle of Le Cateau. The allies were under great pressure from the invading Germans and a strategic retreat was agreed. By 27 August , the British and French had withdrawn to a line south of the River Somme.

There were, of course, many British casualties in these early battles and actions; but other soldiers were killed back on British soil. On 24 August, Private Charles Reeves, who was 21 years old, of the 3rd (City of London) Royal Fusiliers, was on guard duty on a railway line near Winchester when a passing train coming out of a tunnel struck him. He was killed instantly.

August did not end well for the allies. On the final day of the month, Amiens fell to the Germans. What everyone had originally thought would be a quick war, over by the end of the year, was beginning to prove itself nothing of the kind.

Early September saw the end of the retreat from Mons. On 6 September, the Battle of the Marne began. It signalled an Allied advance and was to last until 12 September. In Winchester, the newspapers printed the first lists of casualties but in this early period, perhaps implying that the common soldier was somewhat insignificant, only officers were listed. So, for example, the name of Lord Hawarden, a Second-Lieutenant in the Coldstream Guards, educated at Winchester, was listed as killed in action.

In October, another lieutenant, Walter Edward Hill, was also listed. He was the only son of Mrs Rowland Hill, of 68 Kingsgate Street, and was 22 years old when he died. That same month saw news that the Germans had taken Antwerp on the 10th and, just nine days later, on 19 October, a new battle opened, named after a quiet

Belgian town that would soon become notorious for slaughter and sacrifice. That town was Ypres and the first bloody battle there would last until 22 November.

Also in October, the people of Winchester read that Major F Playfair, who commanded the depot in the city, had been given command of the 1/4 R Hampshire Regiment and that he and his men would soon be leaving for India.

November saw some terrible news for one Winchester family. William and Sarah Freemantle of Easton, Winchester, had twin 26-year-old sons named Thomas and James. Both had joined the 1st Battalion of the Scots Guards and were killed on the same day, 11 November, at Ypres. Neither of the bodies were ever recovered from the battlefield and so they have no known grave.

Also in November, Dr W Prendergast, the organist at Winchester Cathedral, wrote a lively patriotic song entitled *Across the Channel*. This was sung to some of the troops in the city, who joined in the chorus enthusiastically.

In December, on the 14th, an inquest opened in the city concerning the death of another soldier, Company Quartermaster Sergeant James William Guerin, who was found unconscious at the side of the railway line at the bottom of a forty feet high embankment on Friday, 11 December. Guerin never recovered consciousness and died the following day from the effects of a fractured skull. It was believed that he had simply fallen down the embankment in the darkness.

On 16 December, Winchester received a Royal visitor, no less a personage than King George V himself. He travelled to the city from Waterloo Station to inspect the troops based there. He was accompanied by Earl Kitchener, the new Secretary of State for War; the two distinguished visitors returned to London after enjoying a pleasant lunch.

Much was made in the newspapers about the Christmas Truce between the British and the Germans. It is true that this did occur on various parts of the line. One of the battalions involved was the 1st Hampshires but the event did not occur all along the line of trenches. Early in the new year the Collard family of Winchester received a letter from their son, Patrick, who reported that it certainly had not happened where he was serving. He noted that; 'The sniping went on just the same; in fact, our captain was wounded, so don't believe all you see in the papers.'

When hostilities broke out, many in England had believed the war would be a short if bloody affair. By the end of 1914 it was clear that the fighting would likely be measured in years, not months.

CHAPTER 4

Winchester as an Army Depot

The winter of 1914 was a bitter one. When war was declared, a large camp was set up at Morn Hill, east of Winchester. Initially two British divisions were billeted there in tents. So cold did it become that very soon the camp had to be abandoned and the troops were found alternative billets in the city itself.

Once conditions had improved, Morn Hill was re-established as a permanent camp and grew in size through the years 1915 and 1916. Rather more adequate accommodation in the form of wooden

The original tented camp at Morn Hill.

The hutted camp at Morn Hill.

The main road through Morn Hill Camp.

Winchester Barracks.

huts were built along with stables, garages, a cookhouse and even a cinema. Many thousands of troops from Britain and her overseas dominions and colonies passed through the camp until 1917, when the United States entered the war on the Allied side. Morn Hill was then transferred to the Americans, who also used it as a transit camp.

After the war it was stated that over two million men had passed through the Winchester camps during the war, a time when the population of the city itself was only around 20,000. Seven hundred thousand of those troops were from the period after the camp was handed over to the United States. At that time a large military hospital was also built at the camp and it is estimated that in all around 500 men died there, mostly from illness rather than war wounds.

Though many of the troops who passed through Morn Hill and other camps close to Winchester were from Canada, Australia, New Zealand, India and the United States, this chapter will detail many of the British units that were based in Winchester during the war.

Training at one of the camps.

The King's Royal Rifle Corps

3rd Battalion and 4th Battalion – At the outbreak of war they were in India but they embarked for England on 16 October 1914 and were based at Winchester. They embarked from Southampton and landed at Le Havre on 21 December.

5th and 6th (Reserve) Battalions – In Winchester at the declaration of war. They moved to Sheerness area on 9 August, where they remained for the duration.

7th Battalion – Formed at Winchester on 19 August 1914. Moved to Aldershot and then to Grayshott in November. Landed at Boulogne in February 1918.

8th Battalion – As with the 7th; landed at Boulogne in April 1918.

9th Battalion – As with the 7th; to Aldershot in November 1914. Landed at Boulogne in April 1918.

10th Battalion – Formed at Winchester on 14 September 1914 and to Blackdown in February 1915. Landed at Boulgone in July 1915.

11th Battalion – As with the 10th.

12th Battalion – Formed at Winchester on 21 September 1914. Moved to Bisley in November 1914. Landed at Boulogne in July 1915.

13th Battalion – Formed at Winchester on 7 October 1914 and later moved Wendover. Landed at Boulogne at the end of July 1915.

The Rifle Brigade

4th Battalion – In India at the outbreak of the war. Sailed for England in October 1914 and landed at Devonport on 18 November and moved to the Magdalen Hill Camp in Winchester. They were sent to France on 21 December and transferred to Salonika in November 1915.

5th and 6th (Reserve) Battalions – At Winchester in August 1914. In November moved and almost immediately sent to the Isle of Sheppey, where they remained for the rest of the war.

7th, 8th and 9th Battalion – Formed at Winchester on 21 August 1914. They moved to Aldershot in November 1914 and landed in France in May 1915.

10th Battalion – Formed at Winchester in September 1914. They moved to Blackdown in February 1915 and to France in May.

11th Battalion – As with the 10th; to Stonehenge in April 1915 and to France in July.

12th Battalion – As with the 11th.

13th Battalion – Formed at Winchester in October 1914. In November moved to High Wycombe, in April 1915 to Andover and to France in July that year.

The Hampshire Regiment

3rd (Reserve) Battalion – In Winchester in August 1914. Moved to the Isle of Wight in January 1915. It remained there throughout the war.

1/4th Battalion – In Winchester in August 1914. It sailed for India on 9 October. To Mesopotamia in March 1915.

3/4th Battalion – Formed in Winchester in March 1915 and moved to Bournemouth in the autumn. It stayed in the United Kingdom throughout the war, ending the war in Belfast.

10th Battalion – Formed at Winchester in August 1914 and moved to Dublin soon afterwards. Sailed for Gallipoli in July 1915 and then to Salonika on the 6 October 1915.

11th Battalion (Pioneers) – As with the 10th; to Aldershot in September 1915 and landed in France on 18 December 1915.

12th Battalion – Formed at Winchester in October 1914 and in November moved to Codford, and then to Basingstoke, Bath and Sutton Veny in the next twelve months. In September 1915 to France and in November 1915 to Salonika.

The London Regiment

3/13th Battalion – Formed in London in December 1914 and initially moved to Richmond. In January 1916 they were sent to Winchester. They moved back to Richmond in April 1916 and stayed in Britain throughout the war.

The Surrey Yeomanry

1/1st Surrey Yeomanry – Moved to Kent in August 1914. A Squadron moved to Winchester on 21 November 1914 and moved to France with the 27th Division. Other squadrons served in France, Gallipoli and Salonika.

The Duke of Cornwall's Light Infantry

2nd Battalion – They were part of the garrison in Hong Kong at the outbreak of war. On their return to England in early November they were based at Winchester. They landed at Le Havre on 21 December and at the following year were sent to Salonika.

The Welsh Regiment

10th Battalion (1st Rhondda) – Raised in the Rhondda in September 1914 by the local Member of Parliament, Mr D Watts Morgan. Moved to Winchester in August 1915 and landed at Le Havre that December.

The Argyll and Sutherland Highlanders

1st Battalion – In India in August 1914; returned to England and landed at Plymouth on 19 November and moved to Winchester. On 20 December, they landed at Le Havre and moved to Salonika in December the following year.

The Worcestershire Regiment

1st Battalion – In Cairo, Egypt when war was declared and returned to England, landing at Liverpool on 16 October, after which they were based at Hursley Park in Winchester. They landed in France on 6 November.

The East Yorkshire Regiment

2nd Battalion – In Kamptee, India in August 1914 and returned to England, landing in December and were based at Hursley Park. They landed in France on 16 January 1915 and were moved to Salonika (via Alexandria) in November.

The West Somerset Yeomanry
1/1st West Somerset Yeomanry – Moved to Winchester in August 1914 but almost immediately moved on to Colchester. They were sent to Suvla Bay in Gallipoli on 24 September and later served in Egypt, Palestine and France.

The Cheshire Regiment
2nd Battalion – In India in August 1914, they returned to England landing at Devonport on Christmas Eve1914 and were based at Winchester. Landed in France on 17 January 1915, and in October moved to Salonika via Egypt.

The Royal Irish Fusiliers
2nd Battalion – In Quetta, India in August 1914, returned to England and arrived at Winchester on 20 November. Almost exactly a month later, on 19 December, they landed in France. In November 1915 they went to Salonika and went on to serve in Egypt and Palestine.

The Northamptonshire Yeomanry
1/1st Northamptonshire Yeomanry – Moved to Winchester in October 1914 and sent to France on 4 November. It served in France and Italy.

The Northamptonshire Regiment
2nd Battalion – In Egypt at the outbreak of war, they returned to England in October and moved to Hursley Park. They were sent to Le Havre on 5 November.

The King's (Shropshire Light Infantry) Regiment
2nd Battalion – In Secunderbad, India in August 1914 and returned to England, landing at Plymouth in November. Based at Winchester, they were sent to France on 21 December. They moved to Salonika, arriving on 4 September 1915.

The East Surrey Regiment
2nd Battalion – In India when war broke out; they landed at

Devonport on 23 December and moved to Winchester. They landed in France on 19 January 1915 and moved to Salonika via Egypt in October 1915.

The Somerset Light Infantry
3/4th Battalion – Formed in March 1915 and moved to Hursley Park in September 1916 on amalgamation with the 3/5th. The following month they moved to Bournemouth and remained in England throughout the war.

The Queen's Own Cameron Highlanders
2nd Battalion – Based in Poona, India in August 1914, they landed at Devonport on 16 November and moved to Winchester. They were sent on to France on 20 December. They arrived in Salonika on 5 December 1915.

The South Wales Borderers
10th Battalion (1st Gwent) – Raised at Brecon in October 1914, they were moved to Hursley Park in July 1915 and, then, to Hazeley Down. They landed in France on 4 December 1915.

The YMCA hut at Hazeley Down Camp.

The South Lancashire Regiment

6th Battalion – Formed at Warrington in August 1914. They moved to Winchester in January 1915 and to Blackdown the following month. They sailed for Gallipoli in June 1915. They went on to serve in Egypt and Mesopotamia.

The Gloucestershire Regiment

2nd Battalion – In China when war was declared, they returned to Southampton on 8 November. Based at Winchester, they landed in France on 18 December and moved to Salonika in November 1915.

The Middlesex Regiment

3rd Battalion – At Cawnpore, India, in August 1914; they returned to England in December and were based at Winchester. They landed in France on 19 January 1915. They set sail for Salonika on 2 December 1915.

The West Yorkshire Regiment

2nd Battalion – In Malta in August 1914, they returned to Southampton on 25 September when they were based at Hursley Down camp. They landed in France on 5 November.

The Leinster Regiment (Royal Canadians)

1st Battalion – In Fyzabad, India at the outbreak of war, they returned to Plymouth on 16 November and were sent to Winchester. They landed in France on 20 December and sailed for Salonika on 11 December 1915, going on to serve in Egypt and Palestine.

The Royal Berkshire Regiment

2nd Battalion – In Jhansi, India in August 1914, they landed back in England on 22 October and were based at Winchester. They landed in France on 5 November.

The Sherwood Foresters (Nottinghamshire and Derbyshire) Regiment
10th Battalion – Formed at Derby in September 1914, they were moved to Winchester in June 1915 and from there landed in Boulogne on 14 July.

The Hampshire Yeomanry
1/1st Hampshire Yeomanry – Mobilized at Winchester in August 1914, they were moved to defend Portsmouth. They were split up in March 1916 and sent to France, acting as divisional cavalry. The regiment was reunited in January 1917.

The Royal Wiltshire Yeomanry
1/1st Royal Wiltshire Yeomanry – Moved to Sussex in September 1914, where they were split up into independent squadrons, one which was based in Winchester. It moved to France in December 1915. It was reunited in late 1916 and was dismounted and amalgamated in September 1917.

The Devonshire Regiment
3/4th Battalion – Formed at Exeter on 25 March 1915 and sent to Bournemouth in August. They moved to Hursley Park on 1 September 1916 and remained in the United Kingdom throughout the war, ending it in Ireland, where it moved in April 1917.

3/5th Battalion – Formed at Plymouth and then as for 3/4th Battalion.

3/6th Battalion – Formed at Barnstaple and then as for 3/4th Battalion.

Queen's Own Yorkshire Dragoons
1/1st A Squadron – Sent to Winchester as divisional cavalry and then on to France in July 1915.

The South Staffordshire Regiment
8th Battalion – Formed at Lichfield in September 1914. They first

moved to Wareham and after various moves arrived in Winchester in June 1915. They landed at Boulogne on 14 July of that year and were disbanded in February 1918.

The Border Regiment
7th Battalion – Formed at Carlisle on 7 September 1914. They were sent to Andover in December and moved to Winchester in June 1915. They landed at Boulogne on 15 July.

The King's Own Scottish Borderers
7th Battalion – Formed at Berwick in September 1914 and initially based at Bordon. In February 1915 they were billeted at Winchester and in April moved to camps on Salisbury Plain. They landed in France in 10 July 1915.

The East Lancashire Regiment
6th Battalion – Formed at Preston in August 1914, they were initially sent to Tidworth but moved to Winchester in January 1915. From there they moved in February to Blackdown and sailed from Avonmouth on 16 June for Gallipoli. They later served in Egypt and Mesopotamia.

The Royal Welsh Fusiliers
13th Battalion (1st North Wales) – Raised at Rhyl on 3 September 1914. They were originally based at Llandudno but moved to Winchester in August 1915. They were sent on to France in December.

The Cameronians (Scottish Rifles) Regiment
10th Battalion – Formed at Hamilton in September 1914 and based at Bordon. In February 1915 they were transferred to Winchester and from there they were sent to France, landing on 10 July.

The 17th (Northern) Division
A new army division, was formed in early 1914 in Dorset and

moved to Winchester in May 1915. The division went to France in July.

The 28th Division
This was a regular army division, formed at Winchester, at Hursley, Pitt Hill and Magdalen Camps. The division was sent to France in January 1915.

The 27th Division
This was a regular army division that was formed at Magdalen Camp in Winchester in November and December 1914. Sent to France in January 1915.

The 39th Division
This was a New Army division that began to be formed in Winchester in August 1915. It was moved to Aldershot on 28 September.

CHAPTER 5

1915 – Death in the Flanders Mud

1915 opened with a most interesting court case in London, dealing with a crime that took place in Winchester and which received a good deal of local publicity. A gentleman with the rather grand name of Raymond Francis de Lafaye Biard, who titled himself the Marquis de Lafaye, had married a 16-year-old girl named Johanne Home Douglas in Winchester on 28 July 28 1914, but had neglected to tell her that he was already a married man.

It transpired that Johanne, who was the daughter of an eminent doctor, had enjoyed a brief stay in Jersey with her elder sister. It was there that the two young ladies met Lafaye, who charmed them both. However, when he discovered that Johanne was due to inherit £10,000 when she came of age, his interest in her soon grew. A rapid courtship was followed by a marriage in Winchester and it was at that stage that the family decided to report the matter to the authorities, who soon discovered that Lafaye had married one Elizabeth Mary Price in Jersey in 1908 and that marriage had never been dissolved.

The case first came before the magistrates on 8 January, when Lafaye was sent for trial at the Old Bailey. He appeared there on 9 February before Mister Justice Rentoul and was found guilty and would receive a sentence of three years imprisonment. As he was escorted down to the cells, Lafaye shouted to Johanne's elder sister, 'Tell her to wait for me, whatever happens!' She replied, 'I'll tell her. I'll tell her!'

On 12 January, Winchester received another royal visit when the King, again accompanied by Earl Kitchener, reviewed 20,000 troops. The party arrived in the city at 10.30 am by special train and then was driven through the main streets to Chesford Head, where the salute was taken.

What would prove to be an announcement with a very significant long-term impact was reported in the newspapers in February. On the 4th, Germany declared that all the waters around Great Britain would now be considered a war zone. This meant that submarines

The WAR

FOUR QUESTIONS TO EMPLOYERS

1. As an employer have you seen that every fit man under your control has been given every opportunity of enlisting?

2. Have you encouraged your men to enlist by offering to keep their positions open?

3. Have you offered to help them in any other way if they will serve their country?

4. Have you any men still in your employ who ought to enlist?

Our present prosperity is largely due to the men already in the field, but to maintain it and to end the War we must have more men. Your country will appreciate the help you give.

More men are wanted———
TO-DAY
What can you do?

GOD SAVE THE KING.

A typical poster of the Great War. This one was to encourage employers to get their workmen to join up.

Are YOU fond of cycling?

IF SO

WHY NOT CYCLE FOR THE KING?

RECRUITS WANTED

By the S. Midland Divisional Cyclist Company
(Must be 19, and willing to serve abroad).
CYCLES PROVIDED. Uniform and Clothing issued on enlistment.

Application in person or by letter to
Cyclists, The Barracks, Gloucester.

BAD TEETH NO BAR.

Another recruiting poster, this time appealing for cyclists to join the army. Note the interesting comment at the end about bad teeth not being a hindrance.

would attack all shipping within the designated area. The consequences of this declaration would soon be felt worldwide.

On 10 March, a new British offensive in the Flanders region of France opened. Termed the battle of Neuve Chapelle, the battle would rage for three days. Those three days saw the loss of 7,000 British troops, 4,200 Indian soldiers and some 10,000 Germans. It was all for nothing. The initial British breakthrough was not capitalised upon, mainly due to a loss of telephone communications. Over 21,000 lives had been lost, for no real advantage.

Another unsuccessful attack took place on 18 March. This time it was a naval attack by a joint British and French fleet with the aim of forcing the Dardanelles. The attack was effectively repulsed. On the same day, however, some success was celebrated in Winchester when Captain Bell, of the SS *Thordis*, was given a celebratory lunch in the city. Captain Bell had been sailing close to Beachy Head when he spotted a German submarine. The German vessel dived and fired a torpedo at the *Thordis*, which fortunately passed beneath the ship. Bell then turned and aimed his ship at the exposed periscope and rammed the submarine, which was not seen again. He was awarded the DSO for this action.

There was a most interesting sporting event in Winchester on Sunday, 21 March. A cross-country race was organised and made open to all the troops based in the area. A total of 473 competitors entered and ran over a seven and a half mile course, part of the Winchester College's Steeplechase Course. The Mayor of Winchester offered a handsome silver cup for the regimental team winners and other prizes for individual runners. The event was almost a whitewash for the men of the King's Own Scottish Borderers, who claimed six of the first seven places, the winner being Private Gorton, who crossed the finishing line near the Guildhall in a time of 45 minutes and 56 seconds.

The month of April seemed to bring nothing but bad news for those citizens who read the local and national newspapers. On the 22nd, the Second Battle of Ypres opened with the first use of poison gas against Britain by the Germans. It was a series of battles that

The landings at the start of the ill-fated Gallipoli campaign.

included Gravenstafel, Saint Julien, Frezenberg and Bellewaarde; it ended officially on 25 May, through there was fierce fighting in the area for several months afterwards. In all, Second Ypres cost the allies some 70,000 casualties and the Germans about 35,000.

Three days after Second Ypres opened, on 25 April, the ill-fated Allied landings at Gallipoli took place. That conflict seemed to be nothing but bad news from start to finish and would eventually cost the allies possibly as many as 245,000 casualties and fifteen ships, which includes eight submarines; whilst the Turks suffered about 300,000. Of the British casualties some 60 per cent were due to sickness.

The day after the Gallipoli campaign began a secret treaty was signed that would soon become public knowledge in Winchester and throughout the country. Italy, up to now neutral, had agreed to enter the war on the Allied side. For the Central Powers, a new front was about to be opened.

At the beginning of May, a very significant event occurred as a direct result of the German announcement that the sea around Britain was now a war zone. On 1 May, the RMS *Lusitania* set sail from New York, bound for Liverpool, where she was due to arrive on the afternoon of 7 May. At 2.10 pm the ship was roughly 11 miles off Kinsale when she crossed the path of the *U-20*. A single torpedo was fired and struck close to the starboard bow. A second explosion, from within the ship followed and the ship began to sink much faster. As a result, only six lifeboats could be launched successfully and a total of 1,195 souls were lost out of a total number of 1,959. Most of those who died were either British or Canadian citizens, but 128 of the number were American. The event caused outrage in the United States and would, eventually, strengthen the decision for that country to enter the war some two years later.

In Britain the sinking of the *Lusitania* led to anti-German riots throughout the country. Shopkeepers and businesses that had German sounding names, or were run by people of German extraction, were attacked. On Saturday, 15 May, those riots reached Winchester, when a dairy shop, whose manager was believed to be German, was attacked. Goods were thrown into the street by a large mob and order was only restored by a police charge and the liberal use of truncheons.

At around the same time a notice was published advising motorists to avoid the roads between Winchester and Southampton as they were very badly churned up due, no doubt, to the number of troop convoys passing between the two.

More and more men were now joining the forces but the need for labour was as intensive as ever. Women now found their place in the workforce and employed in all walks of life, including farming, as drivers, as tram conductors and most notably in munitions factories. Their work was vital for the war effort; yet another career was added at the end of May when the Home Office announced that 11,000 women were to be employed as police officers. They would undergo special physical training and would be based almost exclusively around large army camp sites, one of

The Germans also had their propaganda postcards. This one depicts Britain as a spider attempting to devour Europe.

those of course being Winchester. As a sign of the times, perhaps, the report concluded with the remark that they would largely be drawn from the middle classes.

June was a quiet one in Winchester, though there were reports

A postcard reflecting the valuable work that women did during the war.

of a youth named John Cousins who was found guilty of a serious sexual offence and was sentenced to a term of five years in a reformatory near Leamington.

There was some good news in July. On the 9th, German forces in South West Africa surrendered. Two days later, the *Konigsberg*, the ship that had sunk the *Winchester* in the very early days of the war in August 1914, was herself destroyed. For some time she had been sheltering in the River Rufigi in German East Africa in waters that were too shallow for the larger British ships to navigate. Two monitors, the *Severn* and the *Mersey* were sent in to sink her on 4 July and set the *Konigsberg* on fire. A second attack followed on 11 July, when the ship was totally wrecked.

Two interesting cases were heard at the Winchester Police Court on 23 July. There had been for some time a fraud perpetrated whereby serving soldiers would inflate the wages they had earned before enlisting. As a result, their dependents were entitled to greater

Another recruiting poster. This time it is the women who are being used to nag their men into the army.

compensation than should have been the case. There were prosecutions throughout the country but these were the first cases heard in Winchester.

In the first, Rifleman Joseph McKenzie and his father, James, were called to court accused of benefiting to the tune of nine shillings per week. The magistrates ruled that there was not sufficient evidence and the case was dismissed.

The second defendant was less fortunate. Rifleman WJ Baggett and his aunt, Annie Emily James, had inflated his wages, though he claimed that another soldier had encouraged him to do so and had actually filled the form in for him, saying that he would certainly not be caught. Found guilty, Baggett was fined ten shillings whilst his aunt, who had received much of the financial benefit, was fined one pound.

In August the citizens of Winchester read the tragic news that the son of the Lord Bishop had been killed in action. Twenty-three-year-old Lieutenant Gilbert Walter Lyttelton Talbot of the 7th Rifle Brigade, the youngest son of the Bishop of Winchester, was killed at Hooge on 30 July whilst leading his platoon into action.

Six days after this, on 10 August, news of another hero was published and this report too involved a member of the church. A letter was published, written by Rifleman S O'Neill of the 1st Royal Irish Rifles who referred to a volunteer padre named Fr Simon Stock Knapp. He had joined the Irish regiment from Winchester as a volunteer and, according to O'Neill's letter, had faced death many times. He was seen hearing confessions from wounded and dying men whilst bullets passed nearby like hailstones. In the eyes of the men the reverend gentleman was not just a hero but a saint and filled them with faith and courage before they went 'over the top'.

In fact, in almost exactly two years' time, the brave churchman would lose his own life on the battlefield. An attack was launched on 1 August 1917 and Father Stock asked if he could over with the men. Permission was refused but he followed them into no man's land soon afterwards and soon found a wounded guardsman. As he was ministering to the injured man Stock was shot in the head and died soon afterwards.

Another soldier died on the railway at Winchester on 27 August but this time, there was no train involved. Private Stanley Roberts, a native of Cheltenham, had been into Winchester with his friend, Private Albert John Savery. At around 8.00 pm both men had enjoyed a glass of dry ginger in the Railway Tavern before leaving to go back to camp by walking along the railway line. They had only gone a few hundred yards when Roberts announced that he had a very bad headache. Moments later he reeled and started to fall. Savery supported him and then lowered his comrade to the ground but he was already dead. The inquest, held in early September, heard medical evidence given by Dr Colclough, who reported that at the post-mortem he had found that Roberts had an enlarged and diseased heart that was the direct cause of his death.

On 25 September, came news that the Battle of Loos had opened. This was the first time the British used gas. It was the largest British offensive of 1915 and the fighting would last until 14 October. The British casualties numbered over 59,000 for the loss of around 26,000 German troops. Commander of the BEF, Sir John French, would face a great deal of criticism over his handling of aspects of the battle and this contributed to his replacment in December 1915.

In October, the citizens of Winchester were shocked to read of the execution of Nurse Edith Cavell in Brussels on the 12th. Since the outbreak of the war she had been sheltering British soldiers and helping them to escape from occupied Belgium. She was arrested on 3 August and admitted that she had helped around sixty British soldiers and others from France and Belgium to escape. Found guilty of treason against the German nation she was shot and, almost immediately, used by the British for propaganda purposes.

11 November, a date that would hold much significance in three years time, saw the British attempt to capture Baghdad, which ended in failure on 22 November. The end of the month saw another Royal visit to Winchester, but on this occasion it was the Queen and Princess Mary who acted on behalf of the King when they reviewed a division of troops.

1915 ended with bad news. On 7 December, the Siege of Kut began, trapping British and allied troops in that city for some weeks. At one stage the besieged soldiers were forced to eat the local cats and dogs after all the horses had been consumed; in the end the garrison of over 13,000 surrendered in April 1916.

On the 19th, Sir John French was finally replaced as commander in chief of the BEF by Sir Douglas Haig. The following day the evacuation of troops from the terrible debacle of the Anzac and Suvla beachheads in Gallipoli was completed; Helles followed on 9 January.

1915 had seen many terrible battles, the use of poison gas and flame throwers for the first time and the loss of hundreds of thousands of men from both sides. Surely things would get better in 1916.

CHAPTER 6

Murder

The execution of Walter James White in 1914, before war broke out between Britain and Germany, has already been mentioned but, with so many men based in and around Winchester and other locations in Hampshire, it can come as no surprise that other murders were committed during the Great War and all involved, in some way, men who were in the army. The city of Winchester played a part in each of these crimes and their stories filled the newspapers in the city.

The first of these tragedies occurred in December 1915. By this time, many troops from the British Empire had landed in England prior to being sent to defend the mother country. By 1915, Grayshott Camp held a large number of Canadian soldiers. On 8 December the Acting Adjutant of the 41st Battalion (French Canadians) Canadian Expeditionary Force, George Codere, called Sergeant Joseph Keller, who acted as a servant at Arundel House where the officer's mess was situated, and told him that he had just killed a man and wanted Keller's help to hide the body. Keller then helped Codere to move the body of the canteen sergeant, Henry Marquis Ozanne, to the cellar of the house. He then helped Codere to clean up some blood and later assisted him in moving the body to the stables and covering it with straw. Codere explained that they had had an argument which had got out of hand.

The matter soon came to the attention of the commanding officer, who in turn informed the police. The body was found the following day by Superintendent Reuben, who arrested Codere and charged him with murder. Only then did the true story come out.

Codere faced his trial at Winchester on Friday, 4 February 1916 before Mister Justice Darling. Mr JA Foote acted for the defence whilst the case for the Crown was outlined by Mr Clavell Salter.

It transpired that Codere had severe financial problems. Edgar Priest, who worked for the Bank of Montreal, where the prisoner maintained his account, testified that on 27 November 1915, Codere's account showed a credit balance of £4 7s 8d. After that date four cheques were presented for payment, totalling £190. All four were returned and the creditors were pressing Codere for payment.

Evidence was then given that the dead man, Sergeant Ozanne, had a large amount of Canadian dollars in cash, which he wanted to change into sterling. When Codere discovered this he told Ozanne that he was going to London soon and would be happy to change the cash for him at a branch of Thomas Cook. Ozanne then handed over the money, expecting to get a sum close to £400 when Codere returned from the capital.

Codere certainly did go to London, for the next witness, Sergeant Alphonse Martin, also in the 41st Regiment, bumped into him at the Savoy Hotel. Codere took Martin to one side and a curious conversation then took place.

Codere began by saying, 'I have something to tell you. I want you to help me make a man disappear. There is a sergeant and he has made a deposit in my hands of five hundred dollars and if you will help me I will divide the amount with you.'

'Alright sir', replied Martin.

Codere continued, 'You will be at the camp and at the door of my room at the Officers' Mess at ten tomorrow morning. When you hear yelling inside the room you will open the door and you will hit the sergeant on the back of the head.'

Thinking that this was some sort of joke or prank, Martin agreed to help but Codere had his concerns and went on to say; 'It is very hard to spill blood. You had better give me some poison. Do you know any good poisons?'

Continuing with the spirit of the joke, Martin named a chemical he had seen in the medical unit and said that a few drops would kill instantly if added to a glass of whisky. In fact the chemical he named was a mild astringent and was not poisonous; but Codere seemed pleased and suggested he would get some. Finally, Codere asked if he would bring a large box to Arundel House so he could move the 'thing'. Codere meant the dead body but Martin believed that the joke was over and the officer actually had some equipment to move. He agreed to bring a box as instructed.

Sergeant Keller told the court that on the afternoon of 8 December, he saw Codere bring Ozanne into Arundel House and pour him out a glass of whisky. He then saw Codere use a rubber dropper to put something into Ozanne's glass. Keller left the room and went into the kitchen but Codere came in a few minutes later and said, 'Don't talk Joe. I have killed a man.'

Keller followed Codere into his room and found the body of Sergeant Ozanne lying in a pool of blood. At Codere's instructions and terrified for his own safety, Keller helped him to clean up and later to move the body. He tried to report the matter later but could not find a senior officer. At one stage, during the cleaning up process, a lance corporal had come in and saw what was going on.

That lance corporal was Louis Desjardins, who said that it was around 4.30 pm when he went into Arundel House to find Codere and Keller washing blood off the floor. He was asked to help but refused to get involved. Later Codere took him down into the cellar and showed him the body of Ozanne lying on the bottom step. Codere then handed Keller his trench stick, which was heavily bloodstained, and ordered him to burn it. Keller put the weapon into the stove. The next morning, Desjardins and Keller reported the matter to Major Gaston Henry Hughes.

Codere, for his part, did not seem to register how much trouble he was in and the possible consequences if he were found guilty. After his arrest he wrote a letter to Keller, in French. When translated the letter was a statement that he knew Keller had killed Ozanne and that if he confessed, Codere would do all he could to get him off. This was not, however, a clumsy attempt to transfer guilt. It appeared that Codere really did believe that Keller had murdered Ozanne for one of the final witnesses was the Roman Catholic priest from Winchester Prison, who stated that it seemed Codere had no recollection of being the person who struck the fatal blows and seemed to remember Keller committing the crime.

On the second day of the trial the jury retired and after an absence of twenty minutes, returned to announce that Codere was guilty. He was then sentenced to death. An appeal was entered but was dismissed on 28 Februar,y despite evidence that Codere was suffering from some sort of mental illness. It was stated that once, while on parade in Ottawa, he had suddenly stopped and thrown a man into a ditch because he did not believe the man had a right to look at his regiment.

In the event Codere did not hang. His sentence was commuted to one of life imprisonment and he was eventually released on licence on 21 February 1930.

The second of these cases occurred in early January, 1916. On the 10th of the month two Military Policemen, Private Henri Jolicoeur and Private Arthur Lamadeleine, both of the 41st (French Canadian) Battalion, walked into the bar of the Prince of Wales Hotel at Whitehill, near Bordon. Almost immediately Lamadeleine noticed that another soldier from his regiment was standing against the bar but was not wearing his cap.

Lamadeleine went over to the soldier, a Russo-Canadian named Private Samuel Sobolovitch, and asked him where his cap was. Sobolovitch replied that it was outside and asked Lamadeleine to help him find it. When he refused and told Sobolovitch to find it himself, the latter walked into the smoking room and was seen to take a large clasp knife out of his pocket. Opening the knife, Sobolovitch returned to the main bar and tried to stab Lamadeleine, who fortunately was able to block the blow with his left arm, though he did receive a cut in his tunic sleeve.

Sobolovitch tried to strike a second time and that too was blocked. As a third attempt was made, Jolicoeur stepped between the two men and received a deep would in his upper right shoulder. Unfortunately the blade severed a major artery and Jolicoeur started to bleed profusely as he fell to the floor, shouting, 'I am injured to death'.

Arrested and charged with murder, Sobolovitch appeared before the inquest on 13 January and before the magistrates exactly one week later, on 20 January. Both courts returned a verdict of wilful murder and Sobolovitch was sent to Winchester to face trial for the capital offence.

This took place on 7 February before Mister Justice Darling. Evidence was given that when he was arrested, rather than showing remorse for what he had done, Sobolovitch shouted, 'Send me a Russian captain! I don't want any Frenchman! Let me have some bullets and I will shoot the lot!'

The court also heard that had Jolicoeur received prompt medical attention, he may well have survived the attack upon him. The first medical practitioner on the scene was an army doctor who applied a tourniquet to the wound and accompanied the injured man back to his camp. Only there was it seen that wound was a very severe one and arrangements made to take Jolicoeur to the nearest hospital. He died in the ambulance on the way.

It was perhaps this knowledge which persuaded the jury to find Sobolovitch not guilty of murder, but guilty of manslaughter. For that offence he was sentenced to one year's imprisonment, with hard labour.

A third murder case occurred at the very beginning of 1917, at Aldershot. Sergeant Leo George O'Donnell joined the army voluntarily in 1914 and was in the Royal Army Medical Corps. At the end of 1916, he received notice that he was to be sent to France and he wished to avoid this at all costs. He came up with what he thought was the perfect escape plan.

In July of 1916 O'Donnell grew close to the daughter of Lieutenant Frederick William Watterson, also of the RAMC who, as Quartermaster, had a large amount of money in his safe. An engagement was discussed and, on the afternoon of 1 January 1917,

O'Donnell asked for Miss Watterson's hand in marriage and she had agreed. In fact, she went out with a girlfriend at around 8.15 pm that evening in order to celebrate, leaving O'Donnell alone with her father. When Miss Watterson returned home, expecting to find her father waiting for her, she was surprised to find the house empty. Later that night the body of Lieutenant Watterson was found in a ditch and nearby was the handle of a lavatory brush which had been made into a makeshift truncheon. Miss Watterson recalled that O'Donnell had just such a weapon, which he habitually carried around with him. O'Donnell was arrested on 2 January and, unable to account for his movements and freely admitting that the lavatory brush truncheon was his, found himself charged with murder and languishing in Winchester prison.

O'Donnell's trial opened at Winchester on 9 February before Mister Justice Darling and lasted for two days. The case for the defence was led by Mr Clavell Salter, whilst Mr Du Parcq led the prosecution for the Crown.

One of the chief arguments for the prosecution was a number of letters that O'Donnell had written whilst being held in Winchester Prison. In each of these he tried to bribe possible witnesses into giving him an alibi for the two hours or so he had been alone with Lieutenant Watterton. One of the letters was to a fellow sergeant named Hesketh, to whom O'Donnell wrote, 'Now Hesketh, for God's sake clear up these two hours for me. Say you saw me at a social or anywhere.' To a bandsman named Izood he penned, 'Help me clear up these two hours. Say you spoke to me at about a quarter to nine in D Block. I will give you £100 when I come out.' Similar letters were written to his intended bride, Miss Watterson, and also to an ex-girlfriend, Miss Walker. All of these letters had been passed on to the police.

In his own defence, O'Donnell tried to suggest that the murder had been committed by two Spaniards claiming that he had seen these two men visiting some months before the murder. After they had gone, Watterson confided in him that he had had an affair with a Spanish woman whilst he was based in Gibraltar and the result of the union was a son. That son was one of the two visitors and demanded money, saying that if he did not get it he would certainly kill his father.

The jury obviously did not believe any of this story, for they took only seven minutes to deliberate their verdict. Found guilty, O'Donnell was sentenced to death. An appeal against the conviction was lost on 12 March and so, on 29 March 1917, O'Donnell was hanged at Winchester Prison by John Ellis, who was assisted by Robert Baxter.

The fourth and final murder that filled the columns of the Winchester and Hampshire pages was that of Vera Glasspool.

Vera was only 15 years old but looked older than her years. She worked as a scullery maid at the Longwood Estate, south east of Winchester; her parents lived at Owlesbury. Vera lived in the servants' quarters at Longwood and went home every Tuesday and Sunday.

On Tuesday, 12 July 1917, Vera left for home but never arrived. Her father raised the alarm and a search finally revealed Vera's body in Feathered Copse, which was just about half way between Longwood and Owlesbury. She had been strangled and there was also a wound in her throat.

The inquest on the dead girl ended on 19 July. Florence Wells, a friend and fellow servant at Longwood, said that on the Sunday before Vera's murder, they had both gone for a walk during which they met three groups of soldiers. Later that day, Vera told Florence that she had agreed to meet two of the soldiers on the Tuesday, the day she was killed. Vera didn't give any names but said that one was in the Royal Garrison Artillery and the other was in the Army Service Corp.

Dr T Decimus Richards of Winchester examined Vera's body at the scene and later performed the post-mortem. He reported a stab wound below the right angle of Vera's jaw. This wound had pierced the large veins of the neck and the primary cause of death was loss of blood. In addition, Vera had the arm of her mackintosh tied firmly around her throat. There was no other evidence of violence apart from a small bruise on the left temple and Vera had not been raped. A verdict of murder by person or persons unknown was returned.

For some time, that was where matters lay until early December, when a soldier, Private William Fenn of the RAMC, walked up to Constable Burrows in Blackpool and said, 'About six months ago I murdered a girl named Gladys (sic) Glasspool, aged fifteen years, by cutting her throat in a wood near Winchester. Her parents live in a village nearby. She was dressed in fawn clothes. I met her four or five times. I want to get it off my mind. I cannot sleep for thinking about it.'

Fenn was arrested and his story investigated. It was soon shown to be a tissue of lies. At the time Vera Glasspool was murdered, Fenn was shown to be in a camp near Bournemouth. He had gleaned what information he had from newspaper reports and, for some reason known only to him, had decided to confess to the crime. He appeared in court on 5 December and was discharged from custody.

The case remains unsolved to this day, but there is one curious twist. On 19 October that same year Charles B Hicks, a gunner, was arrested and accused of murdering a woman named Emily Maria Trigg in a wood in Kent. Eventually the case against him was dismissed but, at the time of Vera Glasspool's murder, Hicks had been based at Winchester whilst serving in the Royal Garrison Artillery, as was one of the soldiers Vera had said she had arranged to meet.

CHAPTER 7

The Horrendous Slaughter of 1916

On 9 January1916, the newspapers of Winchester reported that the last British troops had finally been extricated from the fiasco that was Gallipoli. The war had now been raging for some sixteen months. The casualties had been so horrendous, that the government saw that there would soon be a shortage of volunteers to support the demand of the army. For that reason, the Military Service Act was passed in Parliament and on 27 January received Royal Assent. For the first time, able-bodied men within certain age limits would be liable to be conscripted into the forces.

January saw more local sorrow. During the month an inquest opened on 55-year-old Frederick John Moon, of Little Minster Street in the city. On Christmas Day 1915, he was in Southampton when he was run down by a motor car, and killed. His tearful widow, Sarah Ann, told the inquest that he had been his happy normal self when he left Winchester that day. Evidence was also given by the owner of the car, Captain Dean, and his chauffeur, George William Lapham, who had been driving the vehicle. They both expressed their deep sadness and regret over the incident and the court decided that no blame could be attached to either of them. It was all a terrible accident and a verdict to that effect was returned.

Another road accident at the beginning of February claimed the life of Frederick Levin of the Army Service Corps. He was riding his motorcycle near Winchester when he was clipped by a lorry. He died in hospital later the same day.

Morale was crucially important and many newspapers throughout the country carried articles on families who were doing all they could to help their country. Winchester was no different. On 12 February, readers were told that Mrs Snow, a widow of Fairfield Road, had no fewer than six sons serving in various branches of the Army and that a seventh son had just volunteered.

In wider news, reports were published that the German government had informed the United States that armed merchant ships would be treated exactly the same as cruisers and therefore would be attacked. It could be argued that these attacks upon what were really neutral ships would, eventually, lead to the end of the war. Meanwhile, in Winchester on 23 February, some happy news was published. The wedding of Major JA Butchart of the Royal Field Artillery and Miss Katherine Rivers Fryer, of Worthy Park, Winchester, was announced, along with congratulations from both families.

Another local tragedy occurred in the middle of March when the death of Second Lieutenant George Allan was reported. Allan, a well-known footballer from Scotland, was an officer in the 3rd London Regiment. On 15 March he was a member of a group of men who were being trained in the use of trench bombs. The trench bombs were placed onto a spring loader, the fuse was activated and then the loader would fire the weapon into the distance, similar to the clay pigeon launchers used by shooters. On the day in question, dummy bombs were being used but at one stage it appeared that the fuse had not been activated on one of the bombs. Allan then leaned over the weapon to see if the fuse was faulty when the spring-loaded mechanism threw the dummy bomb directly into his face. His injuries were horrific and he died within ten minutes. It was reported that had the training been at a later stage, when live bombs were used, as many as a dozen men would have been killed.

On the 21st of the month, readers were told of the court-martial of Lieutenant John Learoyd, who also served in the London Regiment. He was accused of refusing to obey an order to proceed to Southampton. Such an order could mean nothing more than reporting to the docks for transfer to the trenches in France and a refusal to go could be looked upon as cowardice. Fortunately for Learoyd, he was able to prove that he was ill at the time and his doctor had told him that he was not fit for active service. He went on to say that he was now fully recovered, regretted his refusal to report to Southampton and was now eager to join his comrades in France. A not guilty verdict was returned.

In April, President Woodrow Wilson replied to the German communication of February, making clear the anger and reaction of the American people on the subject of unrestricted submarine warfare and the fact that merchant vessels could be considered targets. It had little effect on German thinking.

It was not a month for good news. On Easter Monday, 24 April, 1,250 armed Irish Volunteers took up positions in Dublin in what would come to be known as the Easter Rising. The rebellion lasted for six days, during which sixty-four Irish Volunteers, 132 British troops and Irish police and 254 civilians were killed. After courts martial, sixteen rebels were later executed by the British.

At about the same time that the Easter Rising was coming to an end, the British forces that had been under siege in Kut surrendered to the Turkish forces. The siege had lasted for 147 days, and finally ended on 29 April. Around 13,000 troops, British and Indian, surrendered of whom more than half would die in captivity.

It was also around this time that it was reported in the Winchester newspapers that Private James Scott Druckers, a London solicitor who had been conscripted into the army, had been confined to barracks pending a court-martial. He would be facing his trial on two charges: refusing to strip and submit to a medical examination; and refusing to put on a uniform.

On 1 May, British Summer Time was first introduced as a daylight saving measure to help farming production. Most people

The conscientious objector was ridiculed as well as punished. This is one of a series of postcards that could be sent to such men to embarrass them into joining up.

believed that this would be only a wartime measure. On the same day a letter was published from a female farm worker in the Winchester area who signed herself 'Nemo'. She explained that she had been working on a farm since the previous September and had risen each day at 5.00 am. Her duties included milking the cows, delivering up to thirteen gallons of milk, cleaning out the barns and grooming the horses. She had had only three afternoons off in eight months and was paid the princely sum of five shillings a week.

Another letter was published on 6 May, written by a soldier named DS Parkes, who was held in the detention cells at the Rifle Depot in Winchester. He explained that he was a conscientious objector and was awaiting trial because he had refused to give the military authorities any information. His complaint was that whilst he was being held he had been subject to terrible bullying. Sergeants and higher ranking soldiers had pointed loaded rifles at him, a bayonet had been placed close to his heart and he was told that when he was found guilty he would certainly be shot. The newspaper commented that such behaviour was abhorrent but was undoubtedly the work of soldiers whom it described as 'tartars'.

The case of Private James Scott Druckers, referred to in the papers of the previous month, was finally heard. On 19 May it was announced that his trial had taken place during the previous week and he had been sentenced to one year in prison. This had since been reviewed and was now commuted to ninety-eight days' incarceration.

Earlier, on 11 May, an inquest was held at Winchester on Private Havelock Webber, who was stationed at Hursley. Webber enlisted at Exeter on 7 April and was sent to Hursley for training. On 2 May he said he felt unwell and was seen by the doctor who gave him some medicine and ordered him to stay in his hut. His temperature continued to rise and he was sent to hospital but died the same night. A post-mortem revealed that he was suffering from peritonitis and the inquest returned a verdict that he had died from natural causes.

On 25 May, a second Military Service Act was introduced which introduced universal conscription and the month ended with news of the greatest naval battle of the war when the British and German fleets met at Jutland on 31 May.

Early June saw newspapers reporting the details of the battle at Jutland; the figures were staggering. The British, together with their allies Canada and Australia, had deployed 151 combat ships whilst the Germans had ninety-nine. The British lost fourteen ships and over 6,000 men whilst the German fleet lost eleven ships and some 2,500 men. Both sides claimed victory.

In Winchester, later that same month, the death was announced of 70-year-old Judge Percy Gye, who had been the County Court Judge for much of Hampshire. He had been at home when he complained of feeling poorly. He was taken to a nursing home in the city and told that he needed to undergo an operation but died even before the anaesthetic could be administered.

Other deaths were also announced at the military hospital in Winchester. Private Thomas Curtis Rowe, of the Royal North Devon Hussars, survived the Gallipoli campaign but whilst fighting there contracted enteric fever and frostbite. When he was evacuated from the battlefield he was taken to Malta for treatment and appeared to make a good recovery but, back in Winchester, he suffered a relapse and died three days later. He was buried in the graveyard at All Saints Church, Hursley, with full military honours.

Another soldier who died was Rifleman Charles Ward of the 1st Surrey Rifles. Before the war he was an accomplished bantam weight boxer but he died from pneumonia towards the end of the month.

A more famous personage perished at the beginning of June; his death was reported not just in Winchester but throughout the world. On 5 June, HMS *Hampshire* was sailing from Scotland to Russia to take Field Marshal Earl Kitchener and his entourage to a conference there, when the ship hit a mine off the Scottish coast. Of the 650 or so men on board, only twelve survived. Lord Kitchener and all his staff were lost.

Although the British and Indian troops trapped in Kut had surrendered to the Turks in late April, only now were the names of the prisoners published. Men from Winchester were in those lists; twenty-seven names were given, all members of the Hampshire Regiment. Of those twenty-seven, only ten would ever return to England. The remaining seventeen would all die in captivity. They were Frank James Chapman, Lance Corporal Frank Coles, F Elkins, FJ Forder, Archibald Fulford, GJ Goodchild, Charles William Gray, John Hall, Corporal Walter George Harman, Leslie John Jacob, William Lawrence, William George Miles, Frederick Richards, Quartermaster Sergeant Alfred George Shore, G Soffe, William Arthur Turner and WE White.

On 24 June, the War Office admitted that it had made a mistake in the case of Private Albert M Prowse, a farmer's son. He was accused of being absent without leave from Hursley Camp in Winchester. He explained that he had been exempted until 1

December and it took the authorities some time to confirm that this was the case. He was discharged without the slightest stain upon his character.

One other piece of news received was only merited but a small paragraph in many newspapers on that same day, 24 June. It was revealed that the Allies had begun an artillery barrage along a 25 mile front in the Somme area. According to the reports, this was almost certainly the prelude to a large advance.

The Winchester papers reported a cricket match between Winchester College who had played Harrow on 1 July; it was the first time the two schools had met since 1854. It was a very low scoring game, with Winchester being all out for just 58, NA Jessopp claiming a total of nine wickets. In reply, Harrow scored 104 runs, thus winning by forty-six runs.

At the same time as the two public schools were enjoying a pleasant game of cricket, the Battle of the Somme had opened. The troops had been told that the terrible barrage would all but wipe out

Men going over the top during the Battle of the Somme.

A British machine gun in the devastated landscape of the Somme.

the German defences. Though the fighting would last for over four months, this first day resulted in 60,000 British casualties, of whom one third were killed. It was the bloodiest single day in the history of the British army.

On the 16th of the month, Field Marshal the Lord Greenfell represented the King at a service at Winchester Cathedral in memory of the officers, non-commissioned officers and men of the Kings Royal Rifle Corps who had fallen in the war. Meanwhile the slaughter on the Somme continued, with seemingly endless lists of names published in the newspapers detailing those who had been killed, wounded or were missing.

At the end of the month readers were incensed to see reports of the shooting of Captain Charles Algernon Fryatt, who was born in Southampton. In March 1915 Captain Fryatt had charge of the SS

Brussels, a merchant vessel, when it was attacked by a German U-boat, the *U-33*. Captain Fryatt ordered full steam ahead and tried to ram the attacker, which was forced to crash drive. For his action, Fryatt was presented with a gold watch by the Admiralty.

More than a year later, on 25 June 1916, the SS *Brussels* was surrounded by five German destroyers and forced to surrender. The crew, including Captain Fryatt, were taken prisoner and soon afterwards he was charged with sinking a German submarine, despite the fact that the *U-33* was still afloat and on active service. Fryatt was tried on 27 July, found guilty and was shot near Bruges later the same day. An execution notice was posted in German, French and Dutch, the three official languages of Belgium.

August saw continued heavy fighting on the Somme. On 15 September the Battle of Flers-Courcelette commenced, the third phase attack on the Somme. This part of the battle is best

The poster produced by the German authorities in Belgium after the shooting of Charles Fryatt. It is in three languages: French, Dutch and German.

remembered as the occasion on which the tank (in this case in small numbers) made an appearance on a battlefield.

There were more soldiers who died in and around Winchester in September. Two privates, Reginald Taverner and Claud Tuck, were both killed on the Winchester shooting range after the accidental discharge of a rifle. Another private, WA Smith of the Royal Sussex Regiment, who was wounded on 3 September and transported back to England, died at Netley on 27 September. Longer reports were published on the death of a lieutenant, for on 15 September Lieutenant Raymond Asquith, the son of the Prime Minister, was killed in action in France. He was educated at Winchester.

By far the most detailed reports, however, covered the death of Lieutenant Colonel Guy Baring, commanding 1st Battalion of the Coldstream Guards, for he was the Member of Parliament for Winchester. Born in 1873 he was educated at Eton and then Sandhurst and had fought in the Boer War, when he had been mentioned in despatches. He had been elected in 1906 and was killed in action on 15 September, the same day as the Prime Minister's son. His memorial service was on 1 October in the cathedral, where the Bishop of Winchester officiated. Many local people turned out to show their respect. A by-election was quickly called and took place on the 18th. There were only two candidates and the turnout was moderate, at around half of the registered electorate. Major Douglas Carnegie, the Unionist candidate, received 1,218 votes, whilst his opponent, an Independent, Henry Charles Woods, a well-known writer on military subjects, received just 473 votes, giving Major Carnegie a majority of 745.

On 18 November the fighting on the Somme officially came to an end. In four and a half months of carnage the Allies suffered almost 624,000 casualties, the Germans around half a million. The total killed in the battle came to over 300,000.

Earlier in the month an interesting legal case occupied column inches in the Winchester newspapers. An Irishman named Ernest Ferguson, a native of Belfast, had come to England to seek work in October 1915. At the time the authorities were actively seeking Irish workers and had promised them that they would not be liable to conscription. It seemed, however, that the goalposts had been moved somewhat because, after a certain length of stay, such workers were deemed to be resident in England, which meant that they were liable to be called up. Mr Ferguson had been working in the country for some time, was called up in August and, when he ignored that call, was arrested as a deserter. The court eventually decided that he was liable for conscription and into the army he had to go.

The year that had seen so many men sacrificed for so little gain on the Somme and other battlefields ended when Mr Asquith resigned as Prime Minister on 5 December. On 7 December, David Lloyd George became the Prime Minister of a new coalition government, with Asquith and a significant part of the Liberal Party in opposition. It would be for him and his new cabinet to lead Britain and her dominions and colonies into the next year of conflict.

CHAPTER 8

Stalemate – January to March 1917

A most interesting legal wrangle, directly affecting a soldier based at Winchester, occupied the latter part of the month of January 1917. It concerned a writ of habeas corpus directed against the Army.

A Russian soldier named Kauffmann had served three years in his country's army in the early part of the twentieth century and, after his discharge, set up in business in Alexandria in Egypt. On the declaration of war in 1914 he had answered Russia's call to arms, had signed up and been posted to a camp close by. From there he found himself being shipped to England and, transferred to London, was given a piece of paper to sign. This, apparently, was an agreement to join the British Army.

From London, Kauffmann was sent to Winchester for training but the authorities in Russia found out about the matter and failed to see why one of their soldiers should fight for the British when he had already enlisted in the Russian Army. As the case progressed, it was clear that Kauffmann did not understand English and was only able to speak Russian and Yiddish. The writ was granted and the hapless private was freed from the clutches of the British Army.

On the final day of January, an announcement was made by the Chancellor of the German Empire, Theobald von Bethmann-

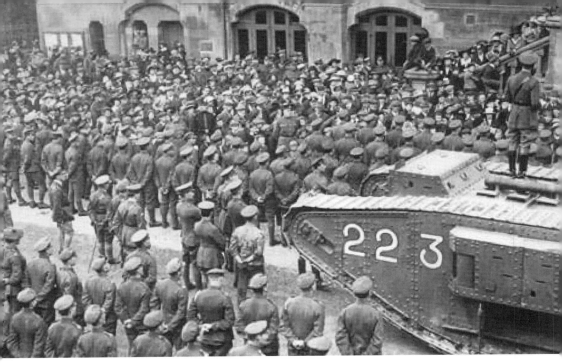

A recruitment drive in Winchester.

Hollweg, that on 1 February Germany would resume unrestricted submarine warfare. This in turn led to a tightening of the tension that already existed between Germany and the United States.

In February, the people of Winchester read of two local deaths. The Reverend WH Lucas, an honorary Canon of Winchester Cathedral, died on 13 Tuesday at the age of 95. Later the same month, Mr Otto Ernst Philippi, a rich and successful agriculturalist and breeder of Hampshire Down sheep, died at Crawley Court in the city. Mr Philippi's wife, Agnes, had died only a week or so before him. A well-loved local benefactor, Mr Philippi had spent a great deal of money equipping the Red Cross Hospital at Winchester in 1914.

In the same month it seemed as if the tide of the war might be turning at last when citizens read that the Germans were pulling back along a stretch of line from Arras to south of the Somme. The euphoria was short lived, however, for all they were doing was moving back to the Hindenburg Line, a strongly fortified position which would give them a shorter front line. In their wake, the retreating Germans did all they could to destroy everything. Villages were razed to the ground, wells were poisoned, roads were blown up and ruins were left booby-trapped.

In early March, British and French troops made a tentative advance after the retreating Germans until they faced their foe in front of the new line. Whatever attacks were organised now would, it seemed, be even more costly in men and equipment.

On 10 March the will of Guy Victor Baring, the Winchester Member of Parliament, who had recently died in battle was published. He left the sum of £49,593 pounds, a very considerable sum at the time.

Some interesting figures were released by the Army on Monday, 26 March and published in the Winchester newspapers. According to the report, the amount of money expended on the war in the year ending 31 March 1916 was a staggering £543,187,548, of which £107,278,448 was for pay. The report also detailed various frauds committed by some soldiers who were sending home parcels containing Army equipment, including blankets, boots and waterproof sheets. In one case, a parcel of clothing worth £207 was sent from Southampton to Winchester, where it was signed for by a Corporal Barnes. The parcel was never seen again and the mysterious Barnes could not be traced.

Perhaps one of the most serious incidents was the complete loss of an entire troop of mules. These had been tethered at Bordon Camp but had apparently escaped from their tethers. They had vanished and their value was put at £1,600.

CHAPTER 9

April 1917, America Enters the War

Though it could not be justifiably said that the entry of the United States into the war directly caused the war to come to a conclusion, it did precipitate a series of events that led to the ultimate defeat of Germany and her allies.

It was only in April that the people of Winchester read about the events that led up to the United States entering the war; they had, in fact, started in January 1917, for it was then that the notorious Zimmerman telegram was sent.

The telegram was a coded message sent by the German Foreign Secretary, Arthur Zimmermann, to the German ambassador in Mexico, Heinrich von Eckardt. Sent in anticipation of the resumption of unrestricted submarine warfare at the beginning of February, it told Eckardt that if this resumption seemed likely to cause the United States to consider entering the war, he was to approach the Mexican Government with a proposal for a new military alliance. The telegram went on to say that Germany would offer all the aid that Mexico would need in an attempt to recover territories that had been lost to the United States.

The telegram was intercepted by the British, decoded and a translation given to the Americans.

When the President, Woodrow Wilson, read the telegram and also took into account that American ships would be targets as a consequence of unrestricted submarine warfare, the details were put before Congress. As a result, on 6 April 1917, a formal declaration of war was made.

It would, of course, take a long time for the Americans to mobilise and send troops to Europe and it was this fact which would dominate German thinking and planning in the next months.

As the people of Winchester read of these events, other more local and rather more mundane matters were also published. Thus, for example, details of Mr Otto Philippi's will were given, showing that he left the sum of £184,058. There was also news of a rather sordid case at the Winchester Quarter Sessions. On 16 April Corporal James Harold Jago pleaded guilty to stealing articles to the value of £7, which were the effects of dead and wounded soldiers. Jago was wounded in battle and sent back to England where, after he had received treatment, he was sent to the Rifle Depot at Winchester and given an office job. His duty was to check the contents of parcels sent home to relatives after a soldier had died or been wounded and Jago simply took some of the property for himself. Despite his admission of guilt the crime was looked upon as so heinous that he received a sentence of eighteen months with hard labour.

Also in this pivotal month the Battle of Arras opened. It would last until 16 May; as so often initially successfully, the Germans rallied effectively. Haig felt obliged to continue the battle long after it was supposed have ended because of urgent retreats by the French, whose own Nivelle Offensive had become something of a disaster. On a per diem basis, Arras was the bloodiest battle of the war thus far for the British.

CHAPTER 10

May to December
1917

There was bad news for one Winchester family at the beginning of May. A young man named Blandford lived in Winchester with his parents at 14 St John's North but in 1911 emigrated to Canada to build a new life for himself. As soon as war was declared, however, he had enlisted in the Canadian Army and had come back to Britain as part of the Canadian Expeditionary Force. His parents were informed, in early May, that their son had been killed in action on 9 April.

Later in the month another Member of Parliament was killed on the Western Front. This time it was Major Valentine Fleming, the member for South Oxfordshire; it brought back memories of the loss of Guy Baring, the local member. In fact, during the war a total of twenty-four members of the House of Commons were killed; one in 1914, seven in 1915, six in 1916, four in 1917 and six in 1918.

On 12 May, a rather more mundane piece of news was of yet another case in the local magistrates' court. Alfred Stroud, who was employed by a firm of Winchester carriers, was charged with allowing his steam-driven vehicle to remain stationary, thus blocking the highway. He was fined forty shillings and costs.

In June the first contingent of American troops, under the

command of General Pershing, landed in France though they would not see action until they had received some training.

On the 7th of the month, the battle of Messines Ridge, just to the south of the Ypres Salient, opened with a monstrous bang, caused by the firing of nineteen large mines. It would last for seven days. It was an important prelude to a planned larger battle that would follow the next month and was a convincing victory that caused the German High Command some concern. This prelude cost the British (along with Australians and New Zealanders) over 24,500 casualties and the Germans a roughly similar number.

Another local casualty was announced in the Winchester newspapers. Charles Freeman, who was aged 23, had worked at the local branch of the Capital and Counties Bank before he answered the call to arms and enlisted in the Royal Fusiliers in 1915 and had recently been promoted to lance corporal. He was killed in action on 12 June during the Battle of Messines.

Perhaps the cost of this terrible war was summed up by no more than a column inch in the Winchester newspapers of 21 July. It noted the stark announcement that some 2,100 old boys of Winchester College had enlisted and of that number 339 had been killed. It was suggested that a cloister memorial should be erected at a cost of some £25,000.

Four days after this, on the 25th, another report showed that there had been a good deal of trouble in Salonika, with many men refusing to obey orders. These had been court-martialled and sent to various prisons. No less than fifty of these men were now languishing in Winchester Prison, serving sentences as long as ten years in some cases.

In Belgium, on 18 July, a massive bombardment of the German lines opened. This was the initial part of a new major Anglo-French offensive. Officially it would be called the Third Battle of Ypres but this offensive, officially lasting between 31 July and 13 November, has become better known as Passchendaele. This was a village situated on the top of a dominant ridge. Its capture took up much of the last six weeks or so of the offensive and involved troops from

Canada, Newfoundland, Australia, New Zealand as well as from all parts of the British Isles. It was notorious for the dreadful conditions, in part a consequence of an exceptionally wet July and August.

Whilst men were dying at Ypres in August 1917 a curious anecdote was published in Winchester. In the late 1890s Donald Nicoll was working on a farm at Barton Stacey and lost his gold watch and chain. All efforts to find the valuable timepiece were in vain and it was believed that the watch had gone forever. Now, on 3 August 1917, a young lad working on the farm, now owned by Mr ET Judd, turned over a sod in a field only to find gold glinting up at him. The find was indeed the watch, missing for some twenty years. A few days later it was reunited with its owner.

A very unusual case came before a court-martial at Winchester on 8 September. Two soldiers, Walter George Trim and Frederick Warnes, were charged with conduct tending to assist German prisoners to escape from a detention camp. Both men pleaded not guilty.

It transpired that the two defendants had become friendly with two German prisoners who worked in the blacksmith's shop. The two men were Paul Schneling and George Noller both of whom had served in the German navy. Taken prisoner, they had first been interned on the Isle of Man but had later been sent to Winchester.

On Saturday, 21 July, Trim and Warnes had gone to a tailor's shop in the city and asked to speak to the manager. When he appeared, Warnes asked the manager, Mr Cecil Salmen, if they could have some paper patterns for suits. Salmen explained that if they wanted suits it would be better to measure them, at which point Warnes admitted that the suits were actually for two German officers, adding that he was sure Mr Salmen would not give them away.

Thinking quickly, Cecil Salmen said that he would come to the camp on 2 August and measure the two men. Reassured, Warnes and Trim left the shop and no sooner had they gone that Mr Salmen was telling the story to the police. Deciding that the two men should be caught in the act, Mr Salmen did indeed attend the camp on 2

August with his 'assistant' who was, of course, a police officer, at which point Warnes and Trim were arrested.

In the event, the court found that Trim had merely gone along to keep his friend company, was not complicit in the crime and therefore a verdict of not guilty was returned in his case. Frederick Warnes was not so fortunate and received a sentence of two years hard labour which was later reduced to one of twelve months.

On 23 October the Winchester Fair took place. The event was well attended and it was reported that high prices had been obtained for sheep and cattle. Ewes were selling for as much as 102 shillings and the best heifers were sold for £42. Very few horses were offered for sale, no doubt due to the fact that many thousands had been requisitioned by the army. It was also pointed out that, possibly due to the war, the pleasure fair was limited to just two stalls.

November was quite a busy month. On the 10th it was reported that Canadian troops had finally seized Passchendaele from the Germans. Four days later, William Clarence Dixon appeared at the assizes before Lord Coleridge, charged with demanding money with menaces. The target of his threats was John Daymond, an official at Winchester Prison. Dixon was described in court as a most deceitful man with a long criminal record though it was also admitted that he had not been in trouble since 1901. Recently he had been offered gainful employment at a weekly wage of forty-five shillings but had turned this down and decided to write a threatening letter demanding £25 from Mr Daymond. Found guilty after the jury had deliberated for just one minute, Dixon was sentenced to three years in prison.

The Battle of Cambrai opened on 20 November and involved the first mass use of tanks. Much ground was gained and indeed the church bells, which had been silenced when the war started, rang out in celebration. However, hopes were dashed and on 30 November the Germans counter-attacked and regained much of the lost ground. This battle cost the British around 44,000 men and 179 tanks and the Germans a similar number of casualties. It was the first time that American troops played a part in a battle, albeit in a minor and support role. On 30 November a detachment of troops working on railway construction behind the British lines was attacked and sustained twenty-eight casualties.

1917 ended on a high note so far as the Allies were concerned, for on 9 December Jerusalem was captured. At about the same time, an article appeared in a newspaper detailing the plight of conscientious objectors. Many of these had been sentenced to long terms of imprisonment and it appeared that some were suffering from the effects of confinement very much. Two men in particular were referred to, both languishing in Winchester Prison. Thomas Gilbert of Sheffield and Douglas Bishop of Tunbridge Wells were both seriously ill, with Gilbert being in the worst condition. He was actually serving his third term of imprisonment and it seemed that, despite his ill health, the authorities simply rearrested him when he was released and charged him all over again, his last sentence being for eighteen months.

Another of the postcards intended to make fun of the conscientious objector.

1917 was a year of stalemate but it was widely believed that the arrival and deployment of fresh American troops in large numbers and unlimited access to American industrial might and presence would finally turn the tide in the next year. The war had now raged for three long years but the general feeling as 1918 dawned was one of hope.

CHAPTER 11

The Lull Before the Storm – January to March 1918

American troops were now pouring into Britain and many of them were based at camps in and around Winchester. On 8 January 1918, President Woodrow Wilson, in a speech to Congress, outlined his famous Fourteen Points as a basis for peace. Soon afterwards, the gist of this statement was published in many British newspapers including those in Winchester. Filled with good intentions and with a model to maintain a peaceful post-war world, once the Armistice was signed the points were gradually watered down. Pursuing his policy was not helped by Wilson's ill health in late 1918 nor by a hostile Senate.

On the 3 January, Driver Charles Sinden of the Reserve Battalion of the Royal Garrison Artillery, based at Winchester, was summoned by Miss Edith Mary Willard, who claimed that he was the father of her child born on 18 June of the previous year. Sinden admitted that he was the father and was ordered to pay maintenance of two shillings and sixpence per week until the child reached the age of 14.

An amusing case was heard by the magistrates on the 29th of the month. Arthur Tratt lived in Winchester but the offence he was charged with took place in Bristol in December 1917. Mr Tratt was one of 400 people queuing outside Mr Webb's pork shop and it was claimed that upon arriving in the shop itself he had used foul language, whereupon Mr Webb told him to vacate the premises as he would not be served. Hearing this, Tratt picked up a slice of bacon from the counter and threw it at an assistant, striking him in the face. A constable on duty marshalling the queue then arrested Mr Tratt and charged him with assault. In his defence, Tratt admitted that he had been angry but only because, after lining up for so long, a woman had elbowed him out of his place at the counter. Found guilty, Arthur Tratt was fined twenty shillings.

In early February the death was announced of 82-year-old Henry Stubberfield. He had been a rather famous cricketer and a member of the Sussex County XI. He was also the cricket coach at Winchester College. At the end of the month, on 26 February, Daniel Hogan appeared before the courts charged with stealing stores from the Americans. For that offence he received six months in Winchester Prison.

March began quietly. Lord Denbigh, speaking in Winchester, said that if a quarter of what the Germans had done in Belgium and France were known then the women of England would see that no conscientious objector would ever show his face in public. That topic appeared in the newspaper a second time soon afterwards when a small, insignificant paragraph reported that 42-year-old Paul Leo Gillan, a conscientious objector who was arrested in August 1916, had died in Winchester Prison.

Two local heroes were praised in the city. Private WG Burnstead of the Army Service Corps and Private S Gregory of the Somerset Light Infantry, both men whose homes were in Winchester, were awarded the Military Medal.

Whilst life was going on relatively tranquilly in Winchester, the high command in Germany had come to a decision. They had heard President Wilson's demands. The British blockade of the ports had imposed a stranglehold on imports of food and raw materials. There were demonstrations in Germany and Austria against the war and soon there would be thousands of fresh American troops to face. It was now going to be a case of acting on the basis of all or nothing. If Germany did not do something decisive to win the war, or at least force a draw, then she would surely be defeated. The decision was made and the results became public all too soon.

CHAPTER 12

Backs to the Wall – March to July 1918

On 21 March 1918, a massive German offensive opened with the aim of splitting the British and French armies. Codenamed Operation Michael, it led to a significant German advance and very heavy casualties for the British and French, who withdrew behind their start lines of 1 July 1916 on the Somme. The Germans also lost similar numbers of men – something they could not afford. On the 24th of the month, British troops evacuated Bapaume under heavy shelling and the town was later occupied by the Germans. This offensive lasted until 5April and was a qualified success for the Central Powers.

On 1 April, as the German advance continued, the Winchester newspapers announced that Mr WJ Chamberlain, previously the honorary organiser of the No-Conscription Fellowship, had been released from Winchester prison, by order of the Home Secretary. Mr Chamberlain had been court-martialled no less than three times and had served 112 days in Wormwood Scrubs and six months in Winchester. On the same day, the Royal Flying Corps and the Royal Naval Air Service were combined into a new branch of the armed forces and was to be known as the Royal Air Force.

On 5 April, Operation Michael ended when it was fought to a standstill. The Germans had captured over 1,200 square miles of

France from the allies. No sooner had this offensive ended than a second one was opened. On 9 April the Germans launched Operation Georgette. The target of this attack was the British line in Flanders. Once again Britain suffered very heavy casualties and a substantial loss of territory. So severe was the situation that two days after this second offensive had opened, on 11 April, Field Marshal Sir Douglas Haig issued his 'Backs to the Wall' message to all British troops.

He wrote;

'Three weeks ago to-day the enemy began his terrific attacks against us on a 50 mile front. His objectives are to separate us from the French, to take the Channel Ports and destroy the British Army.

'In spite of throwing already 106 Divisions into the battle and enduring the most reckless sacrifice of human life, he has as yet made little progress towards his goals.

'We owe this to the determined fighting and self-sacrifice of our troops. Words fail me to express the admiration which I feel for the splendid resistance offered by all ranks of our Army under the most trying circumstances.

'Many amongst us now are tired. To those I would say that Victory will belong to the side which holds out the longest. The French Army is moving rapidly and in great force to our support.

'There is no other course open to us but to fight it out. Every position must be held to the last man: there must be no retirement. With our backs to the wall and believing in the justice of our cause each one of us must fight on to the end. The safety of our homes and the Freedom of mankind alike depend upon the conduct of each one of us at this critical moment.'

Winchester was back in the news at the end of the month when Scotland Yard notified the local authorities of the country that ten

German prisoners of war had escaped the previous night. Three of these were from Evesham, six from Glendavon in Scotland and the tenth was from Flowerdown Camp near Winchester. That same day, 29 April, Operation Georgette was also fought to a standstill, in another substantial gain of territory but once again without achieving its strategic objective. The Winchester PoW, Fritz Ochlke, was recaptured within days.

In May, on the Whit Monday Bank Holiday, a great gathering of the Church Lads' Brigade was held at Winchester. Members of the Brigade came from all over the counties of Hampshire, Wiltshire, Sussex, Surrey and Dorset; all told, there were around 2,000 of them gathered in and around Barrack Square. They were formed up into divisions and marched to the Cathedral where, after a brief inspection, they were dismissed for dinner. After they had all eaten a parade took place, followed by a more ceremonial inspection and the only blot on an otherwise perfect day was the fact that the very hot weather caused a few of the lads to fall out. Fortunately there were no serious casualties.

On 27 May, a third German offensive opened. Codenamed Operation Blücher Yorck this attack was directed at the French front lines in the area of Chemin des Dames, where there was also a British presence. The struggle lasted until 6 June and ended in further heavy losses in men and territory for the French, but, yet again, German casualties were also heavy and, yet again, the Germans failed in their strategic objective.

On 1 June, another conscientious objector was released from Winchester Prison, this time because he was suffering from ill health. Mr GC Williams, a native of Bath, appeared before a military tribunal on 17 March 1916 and was charged with desertion. An appeal was lost on 22 April of that year and a full court-martial followed on 18 July, when Mr Williams was sentenced to 112 days in Wormwood Scrubs. Since that time he had been released from prison three times and rearrested at the gate each time, receiving sentences of six months, 12 months and then another twelve months. It was, perhaps, hardly surprising that his health had suffered so much.

Eight days after this, on 9 June, a fourth German attack was launched. This offensive was directed against the French lines south of Verdun, near St Mihiel and was given the code-name Operation Gneisenau. Yet again there was a massive loss of French soldiers and much territory was lost to the ever advancing Germans. However, it was now halted by a surprise French counter attack, using a large number of light tanks; and yet again no strategic objective was achieved and German losses were seemingly at the same rate, more or less, as those of the Allies.

Perhaps the first glimmer of hope began to flicker.

Even though the French had retreated, they had taken prisoners during the fighting and a German officer, taken close to Verdun, was being routinely interrogated when he commented, 'It is impossible for the war to continue much longer. Our losses are terrifying. My company lost 80 men out of 105. Germany is suffering too much. She cannot go on. We are all tired.' Germany had thrown all she had into winning the war in these last ditch attacks.

Meanwhile, the local news continued. On 18 June, Captain AW Lamond, a Winchester man who had been mentioned in despatches three times, been awarded the Croix de Guerre and who served in the Yorkshire and Lancashire Regiment, married at Roker in Sunderland. Such an event would normally not have made the newspapers but Captain Lamond's new wife was Hettie King, a well-known music hall comedienne and male impersonator. Rather cheekily the newspapers headed the article with 'Boy marries Boy'.

A very sad case was reported in early July. Captain Frederick Boyce Mackenzie had served almost three years at the front, mostly in the Ypres Salient and had now been sent back to England and was based at Winchester. Early in July he went for a visit to the New Forest, something he had done many times before. He met up with some friends and lunched with them and then said that, as the weather was so fine he was going to sleep in the forest that night, again something he had done before.

As he walked into the forest he encountered a local farmer. The two men chatted and the farmer offered Captain Mackenzie a berth in his hay loft, which he accepted. Early the following morning, however, the farmer was woken by a cry of 'Fire!' The hay loft was well ablaze and, whilst a pony was rescued, Captain Mackenzie could not be saved and he burned to death. At the inquest a verdict of accidental death was returned.

On 15 July yet another German offensive, the fifth, was launched east of Rheims. This also was directed against the French, close to the Marne, but this time there was no great advance. The attack stalled and it was the French troops who moved forward. The fighting in this fifth offensive lasted only until 18 July. The Germans were exhausted and now it would be their turn to retreat over the territory they had seized at such a cost.

CHAPTER 13

The End – August to November 1918

On 8 August the Allies began launching their own offensives against the German lines. A combined force of British, Australian, Canadian and French troops attacked the Germans in the area of the Somme where so many men had died two years ago. This time it was the Allies who advanced and much territory was recaptured. Soon thousands of German troops were surrendering and it was reported that over 70,000 prisoners had been taken in just three weeks.

The advance continued into September all along the British front. On the 12th, the Hindenburg Line was attacked and in one of the many battles along the line, at St Mihiel, American forces distinguished themselves.

The day after this on 13 September, a large number of people gathered at Winchester to witness the Duke of Connaught receive the Freedom of the City for his services to the Empire and in his capacity at Colonel in Chief to the Rifle Brigade.

On 15 September, French, British and Serbian troops attacked the Bulgarians at Salonika and gained much territory. On the 19th, another attack was made, this time by the British against the Turks at Megiddo. The Turks were forced to retreat into Syria.

On 27 September, the Battle of the Canal du Nord opened, whilst

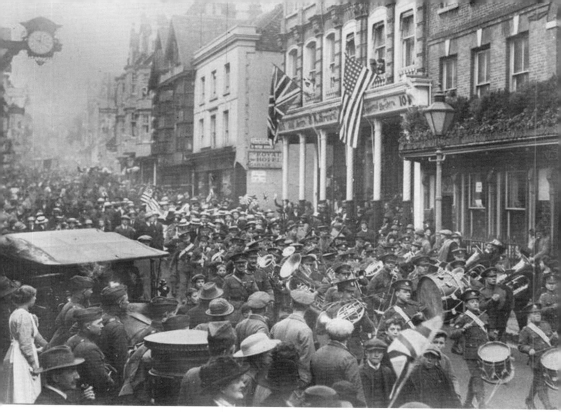

How the Armistice was celebrated in Winchester.

next day an offensive was opened in the Ypres Salient and the Germans were pushed back so that soon Ypres was out of German artillery range..

On 29 September, at the Battle of St Quentin Canal, another hole was punched in the Hindenburg Line. That same day, the German Supreme Army Command informed the Kaiser that the military situation was hopeless. If confirmation of this were needed by the Kaiser he received it the following day, 30 September, when the Bulgarians agreed an armistice, with the Allies.

On 1 October, British and Australian troops, supported by local Arab forces, captured Damascus from the Turks. Meanwhile, in early October Winchester witnessed a most impressive display. A regiment of Czech troops marched through the city with their bands playing and their banners flying. They paraded to the Cathedral where they attended a service after which they proudly sang their anthem.

Kaiser Wilhelm II, who was forced to abdicate at the end of the war.

On 6 October, the first tentative feelers for peace were put out by the Germans, seeking an armistice based on President Wilson's Fourteen Points. Eight days later, on the 14th, Turkey requested its own armistice. The desire for peace spread rapidly. On 29 October part of the German fleet at Wilhelmshaven mutinied and this anti-authority feeling was soon making itself felt across Germany. It seemed that all of the Central Powers were now in a state of utter collapse; on 27 October, Austria-Hungary also asked for an armistice.

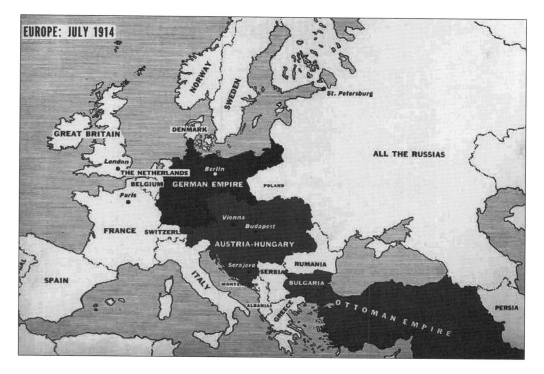

A map of Europe before and after the war.

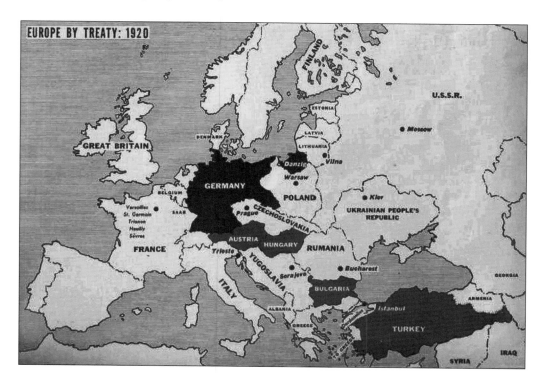

November was to prove to be the decisive month; but still local news was of interest. On 2 November, the author Bernard Capes died at Winchester. He wrote many well-received novels, including: The *Lake of Wine*; *The Jay of Italy;* and *The House of Many Voices*.

On 8 November, William Eason, a motor mail van driver, was sentenced to two years imprisonment with hard labour for stealing four mail bags that contained the property of Canadian soldiers. The following day, 9 November, Kaiser Wilhelm II abdicated and Germany was declared a republic, though the formal declaration would not be signed until the end of the month. The document he signed stated that, 'I herewith renounce for all time claims to the throne of Prussia and to the German Imperial throne connected therewith.'

The formal agreement was signed just after 5.00 am on 11 November 1918 and, was to come into effect six hours later, at 11.00 am. The Great War was finally over.

CHAPTER 14

December 1918

The war had been won. It was time to win the peace. In February 1918 the Representation of the People Act received Royal Assent. For the first time all men over the age of 21 could vote in an election. More importantly, perhaps, the vote was given to women over the age of 30. Women had fought for years to get enfranchisement and it was clear that they fully intended to use this new power.

After the celebrations at the end of the war, the next thing was to decide on a new government and a general election took place on 14 December. The result was a massive win for the Coalition parties, who won 459 of the 707 seats available. Sinn Fein won seventy-three seats, Labour fifty-seven, the Conservatives forty-seven, the Liberals thirty-six and other parties thirty-five. In Winchester, the single seat was a two way fight between two army men, both of whom supported the coalition: Major G Hennessy and Captain WJ West. The result was a win for Major Hennessy by 10,166 votes to 5,569, a majority of 4,597, from a much larger electorate of 32,747, of whom 13,257 were women.

One of the clauses in the armistice had been the repatriation of all Allied prisoners whilst soldiers of the Central Powers were still to be held as prisoners of war. This meant that Britain still had many camps holding such troops. On 22 December, the citizens of Winchester read that three of these prisoners had escaped from a camp nearby. All were wearing civilian clothes so might be difficult to spot. Fortunately, one was recaptured almost immediately and the other two, Hans Young and Wilhelm Harbecker, were arrested in Portsmouth on 27 December.

There was a curious coincidence which seemed to underline the war which had just ended. Hostilities had been precipitated in the first place by the assassination of the Archduke and strangely, it ended with another such crime.

On 15 December, Major Sidonio Paes, the Portugese President, was heading to the railway station in Lisbon so that he could catch a train to Oporto. A man stepped out from the cheering crowd and fired three shots into Mr Paes, who died within minutes. His killer did not survive the attack, for he was seized by the mob and lynched.

CHAPTER 15

The Making of the Peace

Many people believe that the signing of the Armistice on 11 November 1918 was the final end to the war which had claimed so many lives. In fact, as the final clause stated, the initial agreement was to last for just thirty days. In fact, the Armistice was renewed three times before peace was finally ratified. Thus, the First Armistice lasted from 11 November to 13 December, the First Renewal lasted from 13 December 1918 to 16 January, the Second from 16 January to 16 February 1919 and the Third from 16 February 1919 to 10 January 1920. Only then, on 10 January 1920, was the peace treaty finally ratified.

During this period Winchester, like so many other cities, towns and villages, tried to rebuild what had existed before war broke out, but in many ways, things could never be the same. The newspapers, however, carried stories of the ordinary events now that hostilities were over.

In early February 1919, the newspapers carried a reminder of the war, when they announced that Daniel Huxted had been released from prison. Mr Huxted was a conscientious objector who received a four month sentence from magistrates in Oxford but was sent to Winchester to serve the sentence. He had been a market gardener and a member of the Salvation Army but that did not save him from jail. He was finally released on Thursday, 6 February, after a six day hunger strike. It brought home to readers that the prisons of Britain still held a large number of men who had refused to fight on moral grounds. Just because the war was now at an end, it did not mean that their sentences would be suddenly quashed, and many men went on to serve many more months and years inside His Majesty's prisons.

Crime seemed to be one of the main topics of discussion in the newspapers in 1919. Another case, heard at Winchester, was that of Charles William Rose who had killed his two young sons, one aged two years, the other aged two months, at Portsmouth on Boxing Day, 1918. When the case came to court he was found guilty of murder but insane and he was then sent to a secure asylum.

Winchester's new Member of Parliament, Major Hennessy, asked his first question in Parliament when he asked why the restrictions imposed upon clubs, pubs and other places of leisure during the war had not yet been lifted. Mr Bonar Law replied that this matter was being looked into very carefully by a Cabinet Committee.

Education was also back in the headlines. On 3 March Mr MJ Rendall, the headmaster of Winchester College, addressed a meeting at the Victoria Institute in which he described the attributes of the ideal teacher, who would show enthusiasm for boyhood, readiness for responsibility and an acceptance of sacrifice. He added that no teacher deserved the title if his eyes were dimmed by questions of salary, status, tenure of position and the etiquette of the curriculum. In short, he seemed to be suggesting that teachers should simply be grateful for their jobs and not make waves. Curiously, directly below this report was another which detailed that 1,000 teachers in the Rhondda in Wales had just gone on strike for improved pay and conditions and that all the schools there were closed.

On 1 April, readers were told that a large American rest camp at Winchester, through which some 700,000 men had passed, was now finally closed. The last of the men from the camp marched through the city and were given an enthusiastic send off.

Local tragedies were also reported. In the middle of April 1919, a London party consisting of two women and three men were

Another view of the High Street.

enjoying a pleasant motor car drive to Bournemouth when the car came off the road near Winchester and ran up a steep bank. All of the passengers sustained minor injuries but one, Miss Gertrude Burn, was sadly killed.

A more important story appeared at the end of the month that concerned a major riot in the city. Apparently the trouble had started when an American soldier had made a derogatory remark about a black South African soldier who was walking out with a local white woman in the High Street. The South African drew out a knife and made to stab the American but fortunately he was disarmed by the police. No charges were laid but he was warned as to his future conduct.

Far from leaving the matter there, the South African returned to his camp and told his comrades what had taken place. They then armed themselves and within thirty minutes of the first incident, a group of fifty or sixty South Africans, armed with stones and cudgels, were back in the High Street looking for any American soldiers. Another large fight took place and it was with some difficulty that the police finally calmed matters down. Even that was not the end of the riot for that night. Some American troops decided that it was time for their revenge and a large group descended on the quarters of the South Africans. Another pitched battle followed and it was half an hour before armed soldiers of the Rifle Brigade could finally put an end to the fighting.

On 6 May, crime was back in the headlines. The Bishop of Southampton was visiting Winchester and left his car standing at the door of the Holy Trinity rectory. Whilst he was inside some opportune thief made off with his robe case and a portmanteau from the unlocked vehicle.

More army unrest was reported. Originally when men had been conscripted into the army they were signed up for the duration of the war plus six months. The last shots had been fired on 11 November 1918 and the six months would be up on 11 May 1919. There was, however, no sign of the men being demobilised and a group of disaffected soldiers formed a group and distributed leaflets throughout the camps asking soldiers to take matters into their own hands and simply tear off their badges and march out of their barracks on the fateful day. Fortunately, nothing came of this demand and 11 May passed without incident.

Industrial unrest, if it can be termed that, was detailed in the second week of May when Dr W Prendergast, the organist at Winchester Cathedral, spoke at a meeting of the Hampshire Association of Organists. Dr Prendergast complained that the stipend of church organists was very poor and demanded better conditions. He went on to say that the clergy were trained and ordained and surely organists should be trained and licensed. Employment terms should be laid down by the Union and this should include a minimum salary, protection from harsh treatment and a safeguarding of their tenure. He proposed that an attempt should be made to form a National, rather than just a Hampshire, association. This would then give the Union greater strength in their negotiations.

On 17 May, Winchester saw a second riot involving soldiers. On this occasion the trouble started when two soldiers were taken into custody for minor offences, and held in the police station. Their comrades saw this as unnecessary and decided to free them. A large mob, armed with scaffold poles, sticks and large stones attacked the police office in the Guildhall and the Fire Station next door. It was the Fire Station that fared worse, with every door smashed off its hinges and every window broken. Even the fire engine was damaged.

Troops from the Rifle Depot were called out and they restored order at around 11.30 pm when they advanced towards the mob with their bayonets fixed. There were two further arrests, both civilians, and they appeared before the magistrates a few days later. The first of these men, Frank Alfred Milford, of Middle Brook Street, explained that he had been rather drunk and on his way home when he encountered the mob of soldiers. He decided to seek sanctuary in the nearest building, which just happened to be the police station, where he was promptly arrested and charged with drunkenness.

The second man was Edward Carter of Water Lane, who was charged with obstructing the police. He claimed that he too was just passing by and got caught up in the fracas. He denied that he had obstructed any officer. Both men were discharged with a caution.

A story in the papers on 30 May described Otto Hoemke, a German PoW who had just escaped from Morn Hill Camp near Winchester. He was described as five feet ten inches tall, of broad build with a fair complexion and grey eyes. He was dressed in brown trousers with a red patch, a sailor coat and a peaked cap.

The following month, June, saw more military problems, this time at Hazeley Down Camp at Winchester. A number of soldiers who had been prisoners of war in Germany but were now back in England, were told that they were to parade as they were being transferred to another camp. They were not told which camp they were going to and so refused to go on parade. Their complaint was that they believed they were being taken abroad and it was unfair that they should be sent back overseas. They would be happy to be sent to any camp in England but would not go back to France, Belgium or any other foreign country. The report stated that their complaint had been forwarded on to the War Office for consideration.

In 1918, Winchester rejoiced the end of a terrible war. In the years afterwards the city tried to rebuild, as did so many places in the British Isles. It was a time of hope and reconstruction and the people who looked upon the dawn of 1919 believed that they had a future to look forward to; the war to end all wars was over. They could not know that twenty years later, another conflict would engulf the world in a new, even more ferocious, struggle for freedom.

Index